"Building a sense of humor can turn your life around. Feeling less stressful and skipping along the lighter side of life might be the right road for you. Paul's book is your road map."
—*Phyllis Diller, First Lady of Comedy*

"Paul Ryan knows comedy! He is one of the industry's true teachers who knows how to cultivate humor—from hosting, to sitcoms, to improv. Paul pays attention to all of the comedy details that separate the amateur from the professional. He delivers all this to you with a comedy punch in *The Art of Comedy!*"
—*Debra Wilson, actress from* Mad TV

"Paul Ryan knows funny. The time I spent with him in his comedy workshop was valuable and laugh-filled."
—*John Larroquette, Emmy award–winning actor*

"Paul's relaxed style of teaching puts you at ease and allows you to take chances and experiment, without the usual anxiety."
—*Bryan Cranston, Emmy-nominated actor from* Malcolm in the Middle

"A personal and specific approach to acting and comedy. Practical guidance, with exercises that are fun and clear."
—*Steven Nash, Arts and Letters Management; president of Talent Managers Association*

"Paul Ryan is fabulous. I learned so much about comedy from him. Now you can learn amazing comedic skills from the man who teaches comedy to the stars."
—*Sally Kirkland, Oscar-nominated actress and Golden Globe winner*

"Since I'm Korean—and Koreans are the funny people of Asia— I know all about funny. Paul Ryan does, too. He's hilarious, smart, generous, and a great communicator. In fact, we should make him an honorary Korean. I'll get on that. So buy this book and strap on your seat belts for a fun-filled ride."
—*Suzanne Whang, award-winning comedian and host of HGTV's* House Hunters

"What the world needs now is love, joy, and comedy. Just like love and joy, comedy is all about doing, not talking about it. Everyone can benefit from Paul Ryan's *The Art of Comedy*."
—*Dr. Ava Cadell, loveologist and best-selling author*

"If you want to find a long-lasting relationship, you need to develop a sense of humor. With Paul Ryan's method of becoming funnier, you may find your true sweetheart. *The Art of Comedy* could be the book that leads you to the person of your dreams."
—*Renee Piane, best-selling author and founder of Rapid Dating*

"Being funny is an art, but turning funny into success is a skill. Paul Ryan's bullet points and bulletproof techniques are on target for any actor or performer who wants to transform his or her career. His practical exercises in the book will get you laughing all the way to the bank."
—*Neil Bagg, talent agent*

"Paul gives anyone who thinks they might be funny a chance to find out. Valuable exercises will have you entertaining your friends right away. For actors, this can be your key to landing the comedy roles."
—*Judy Kerr, acting coach; author of* Acting Is Everything; *dialogue coach for* Seinfeld

"As a network exec and producer, if I know that you came from Paul's camp, your resume and reel are going to move to the top of the stack."
—*Kent Emmons, founder/CEO of National Lampoon Radio and Studio Funny*

THE ART OF COMEDY

GETTING SERIOUS ABOUT BEING FUNNY

PAUL RYAN

BACK STAGE BOOKS

NEW YORK

Senior Editor: Mark Glubke

Editor: John A. Foster

Art Director: Julie Duquet

Designer: Christopher Cannon, Eric Baker Design Associates

Production Manager: Katherine Happ

Back cover photograph by Bradford Rogne

First published in 2007 by Back Stage Books, an imprint of Watson-Guptill Publications,
Nielsen Business Media, a division of the Nielsen Company
770 Broadway, New York, NY 10003
www.watsonguptill.com

Library of Congress Cataloging-in-Publication Data

Ryan, Paul.

The art of comedy : getting serious about being funny / Paul Ryan.

p. cm.

ISBN-13: 978-0-8230-8467-8

ISBN-10: 0-8230-8467-1

1. Acting. 2. Comedy. 3. Improvisation (Acting) I. Title.

PN2071.C57R93 2007

792.02'8—dc22

2006029058

Printed in the U.S.A.

First printing, 2007

1 2 3 4 5 6 7 / 13 12 11 10 09 08 07

CONTENTS

ACKNOWLEDGMENTS

I WOULD LIKE TO THANK ALL THE GREAT COMEDY LEGENDS WHO inspired me so much growing up in Philadelphia and England. They became my friends on television and in the movies, and made me laugh...the greatest gift anyone can give.

I send out a big thank you to Jeff Black for introducing me to Mark Glubke at Watson-Guptill Publications. Thank you, Mark, for planting the important seeds.

I would like to thank John Foster for his brilliant editing, enormous contribution, and for gracing the book with his magical touches. The skill of an editor is often unrecognized, because the good ones make it look so seamless. John has the ability to take the words and simply make them better.

I send a lot of gratitude to Rick Benzel for helping me lay the groundwork for the book and pushing me to get it done. I send appreciation to Elissa Kerhulas for her consciousness, Monique High for her tutelage, and Carol Green for separating the wheat from the chaff.

Thank you to my wonderful parents, Joyce and Ed Feldman, for doing whatever it was that made me want to be part of the entertainment industry, for all the laughs through thick and thin, and for all of your loving support.

Thanks to my wonderful friends for being there throughout the writing process, including Christine Adzich for her encouragement; Karen Cadle for being the great friend that you always are; as well as Judi Faye, Alex Ranko, Leigh Taylor Young, Frank Mills, Richard Gordon, Bobby Macik, Andy Gross, Jaki Baskow, Rudy Milanovich, Andrea Anderson; fellow L.A. Lakers fan Tracy Martin; Bill Margolin; the "Healthy gang" at Erewhon; Dental geniuses Dr. LanVi Do and Dr. Alan Kaye; my associate Martin Swoverland for his patience; family members Ida and Fred Feldman, Sylvia, Sahl, and Andy Becker, Barbara, Barry, Brandy, and Briana Bond, Maxine Easton, Shirley, Ed, and Maud Burrage. I would like to thank my two dogs, Max and Spirit, for their unconditional love and for proofreading every draft.

Thanks to my students, who have been both students and teachers to me, and who always keep me honest. A big heap of gratitude to all the actors I have ever worked with, who supported me in expanding my comedy talent, and to all the casting directors, producers, and directors that had the brilliance to hire me as an actor. I wish there were many more of you, but fortunately it's not too late.

Thanks to Rev. Dr. Michael Beckwith and my Agape family for loving me and supporting "my funny." My announcement to you is "You guys are beyond awesome!"

Thank you, God, for being my biggest fan!

PREFACE

I'VE BEEN TEACHING COMEDY ACTING AND IMPROVISATIONAL skills for more than twenty years, including thirteen at CBS Studio Center in Studio City, California, home of many top TV sitcoms, such as *Seinfeld, Will & Grace,* and *That 70's Show.* It certainly was great fun to visit and hang out with some of the stars and producers of these shows and to be able to take some of my students to their sets. Over this time, I've taught hundreds of actors throughout the country, including Emmy Award-winning actor John Larroquette of *Night Court;* Bryan Cranston of *Malcolm in the Middle,* who worked on the same lot where I taught; Hal Sparks, former host of *Talk Soup* on E! Entertainment Television; Golden Globe winner Sally Kirkland; Emmy winner Leigh Taylor Young; and many others.

I am inspired and impassioned every time I teach comedy. It is a thrill and a joy to have my students open up, and to help them get in touch with their comedic gifts, especially those who don't realize how much natural genius they have and who only need to learn how to tap into it. My role is to show people how to "mine for their comedy gold"—that resource of rich, valuable, authentic humor that arises from *their* unique personalities and life experiences.

Perhaps my personal comedy journey can inspire you to recognize that anything is possible as you begin your comedy journey. Little did I know when I was a teenager that I would eventually go on to study comedy in the same improv classes with Robin Williams and John Ritter; meet Lucille Ball; act in comedy films with Goldie Hawn, Michelle Pfeiffer, Sir Peter Ustinov, and Tim Conway; and interview Steve Allen, Milton Berle, Johnny Carson, as well as more than two thousand other celebrities on various talk shows that I created, produced, and hosted.

I guess I could say that comedy has been a part of my life since the day I was born of an American Jewish father and an English mother. My genius comedy friend Jackie Mason said to me after meeting my parents, "Your father couldn't find a date in Philly and your mother couldn't find a guy in all of England, thank God they found each other." They named me Bernard Feldman and Bernie for short—so you understand why I go by the stage name of Paul Ryan.

I grew up as an only child, so I spent a lot of time after school with television as my playmate. Characters like Lucy and Sergeant Bilko were my buddies. I watched them so regularly that I could recite almost every episode by heart. I was fascinated by the characters, the banter, but most of all by the laughter these great actors could provoke.

When I was fifteen, my family and I moved to England, which gave me the opportunity to spend a lot of time watching English sitcoms "on the telly." Getting familiar with the British sense of humor, I was on my way to becoming an international devotee of the art of comedy.

I had never acted in high school, but I decided to move to Los Angeles and study theater arts at Los Angeles City College. When I attended my first orientation, I walked onto the theater stage, which was pitch black. I had no idea how to turn on the lights. As I attempted to "feel" my way to the light switch, I fell off the stage and right into the empty orchestra pit. My first time on the stage wasn't "the pits," but rather, "in the pit." Talk about breaking a leg!

I soon became fascinated with the process of acting and began to expand my training. I enrolled in private lessons with the very gifted actress and writer Jenna McMahon, who worked on *The Carol Burnett Show*. Jenna's daughter, Kerry Holden, was my classmate at L.A. City College, and told me her mother had studied with one the greatest acting coaches of all time, Stella Adler. I learned the art of personalizing my acting, knowing what my action is in a scene, and the great benefits of sense memory and observation work.

I trained with Jenna for two years, and her instruction cemented my foundation in the basics of acting. I am grateful for my early work with Jenna McMahon. Her training enormously affected the eight vocations that have defined my career: comedy, acting, teaching, TV hosting, producing, writing, directing, and public speaking. Jenna taught me that *everything works from the inside out*, a principle I will help you master.

After graduating from college, I pursued my studies at Phillip Browning's workshop in Hollywood and continued to improve on the fundamentals of breaking down a scene and working with other students in a professional manner. This benefited me tremendously, since in my classes I continuously partner up actors and actresses to work on scenes. This can be a highly challenging process, as actors have to deal with their egos, frustrations, and fears that come up when doing the work.

I continued my training with the great veteran character actor, Harvey Lembeck, who played Corporal Rocco Barbella on *The Phil Silvers Show* ("Sergeant Bilko"). Harvey's workshop was *the* comedy workshop to attend in Hollywood—and everyone knew it. My class included some unknown actors at the time: Robin Williams and John Ritter; Bill Christopher, who played Father Mulcahy on *M*A*S*H*; Phil Foster and Carol Ita White, regulars on *Laverne and Shirley*; the talented comedy actress Lynn Stewart; Michael Lembeck, the Emmy-winning director of *Friends*; Helaine Lembeck, a regular on *Welcome Back, Kotter*; and Mary Kaye Place, a regular on *Mary Hartman, Mary Hartman*. This class was hilarious. Every Monday night distinguished show biz notables like Jerry Lewis, Norman Lear, and other top Hollywood producers would sit in the back of the theater, laughing their heads off and watching the blossoming talent.

Among my stellar classmates, I was one of the youngest and greenest. I was so raw that Harvey made me audit his class for six months before he gave me permission to officially participate. I was a nervous wreck as I sat through each class, until the day Harvey finally said to me, "All right, Curly. Let's see what you can do!"

My first year in class was very difficult, to say the least. I had already learned a great deal from watching my classmates, yet the level of anxiety I felt in performing was a constant challenge. I threatened to quit a number of times, but some of the veterans of comedy, including actor Roy Stuart, who guest-starred on scores of TV shows, constantly encouraged me to continue. I will never forget their support. It took over a year, but finally, the art of comedy started to click within me. I finally understood the truth that I could use my own persona, be honest in a scene, let the comedy come out of the situation, and open my *own* comedy imagination.

Like nearly every student in Harvey's class, I continued to audition for film and television. My training began to pay off when I landed several roles. My first was in the comedy film *Butterflies are Free*, starring Goldie Hawn. My role was small, but I felt completely comfortable working with someone of Goldie's caliber. My next film was *The Affair*, in which I co-starred with Natalie Wood and Robert Wagner. We were a small cast, and due to my improvisational training, I was able to work closely and comfortably with these more-experienced actors who were at the top of their game. I then landed a role co-starring in *Charlie Chan and the Curse of the Dragon Queen*, in which I got to act with an all-star cast, including Peter Ustinov, Lee Grant, Angie Dickinson, Richard Hatch, Brian Keith, Roddy McDowall, and Michelle Pfeiffer. I also did some TV guest appearances on various sitcoms and comedic movies of the week.

After a year of studying with Harvey, another opportunity arose from his class that changed my life. When Harvey's assistant left to work on *The Captain*

Kangaroo Show, I shined at his good-bye roast. Harvey hired me on the spot to become his new assistant, and I began to teach some of his workshops and substitute for him when he was out of town. I appreciate that Harvey saw the teaching potential in me, and I will always be very grateful for his belief in me. He inspired me to invent, create, and write many new improvisational exercises and sketches, which I continue to use today in my classes.

A few years after Harvey departed Earth (undoubtedly to establish a heavenly comedy class), I decided to open my own comedy school, due to my love of teaching comedy. I began offering classes at the Coast Playhouse in Hollywood, and my reputation as a comedy teacher started to soar.

One of my early students was John Larroquette, who had been focusing on heavy drama. While John had a penchant for Eugene O'Neill's *Long Day's Journey into Night*, he wanted to change his direction toward comedy, and his manager encouraged him to attend my classes. John had enormous raw talent, and it was an absolute pleasure to help him explore his new path. He was eventually cast in the extremely successful TV sitcom *Night Court*, a show on which I guest starred. John continues to this day to be a superb comedic actor, and it's always a joy to talk to him when we meet at a Hollywood function.

My comedy school became successful, and in 1993 I moved to CBS Studio Center for thirteen years. Today, I train dozens of actors, teachers, writers, stand-up comics, public speakers, and anyone who wants to develop a lighter, more joyful, comedic side to his or her personality. I teach all levels— beginning, intermediate, and advanced. Many of my students stay with me for years, honing their skills and deepening their search for comedy gold. I have a continuous flow of students who benefit from the wide range of improvisational experiences my classes give them. I have had scores of students land work on TV commercial campaigns, TV shows, major movies, voice-overs, and Broadway, and some who have even become regulars on TV sitcoms.

I present workshops and classes throughout the United States and abroad. I have taught comedy acting workshops in New York City, Philadelphia, Las Vegas, Orlando, Miami, Vancouver, and Toronto, and was hired to be the comedy consultant for the first TV sitcom in Norway, as well as the comedy coach for a Dutch comedy film.

There's another part of my career that I'd like to share with you, because it speaks volumes to how your training in comedy acting can open other avenues for you, as it did for me.

In June 1977, I had an idea for a TV show. After gathering the courage to call a local cable television station, I said, "I want to host a talk show."

Much to my surprise, they replied, "Sure. When would you like to start?" I didn't know what they were talking about, but they were referring to something called public access television. I simply fell into it. The call led to *The Paul Ryan Show,* a thirty-minute talk show in which I interviewed celebrity guests. The show lasted two and half years on a local Los Angeles cable television station. My guests included some of the top names in Hollywood, such as Jack Lemmon, Sophia Loren, Henry Fonda, Michael Caine, Dudley Moore, and many more—a total of 236 guests. I learned about Hollywood by interviewing Hollywood, as my guests included producers, directors, stars, and many other film and television notables.

As an interview host, I aimed to have substantive and meaningful conversations with my guests, not gossipy chitchat. The celebrities appreciated talking to me, and were grateful that I took the time to learn about them, study their careers, and discuss important professional issues about acting and directing.

Fortunately, my show was so successful that I was asked to expand it into a national TV cable show, also called *The Paul Ryan Show.* I ended up doing another 270 episodes, again interviewing one Hollywood notable in each show. Three years later, I became the series co-host of *Mid-Morning L.A.* with actress/host Meredith MacRae. Following this, I became a celebrity correspondent for *Entertainment Tonight,* and went on to host and produce 175 shows around the world for the Travel Channel.

I feel blessed to have had so many opportunities in my life to follow my bliss, including my love for comedy. I am fortunate to have trained with many of the top acting coaches and comedy teachers in the country, and to have taught some of the best comedic talent the entertainment world has ever known. I also feel honored to have had the opportunity to interview more than 2,000 celebrity guests, who allowed me to learn from them.

I decided to write this book because I hope that many people can benefit from my expertise, training, and guidance. I'd love for you to move to Los Angeles and take my classes, but I know most of you simply cannot, so sharing my expertise with you in this book is the next best thing.

The following chapters will cover everything I have spent years learning and perfecting in order for *you* to be successful in comedy. I am committed to making a difference in your comedy journey, an experience that could change your craft—and possibly your life—forever. All you need is the desire, commitment, passion, and interest in fully expressing your comedic gifts. Are you ready?

INTRODUCTION

IF YOU ANSWER "YES" TO ANY OF THE QUESTIONS BELOW, YOU'VE picked up the right book:

- Are you an actor dreaming of landing a juicy role on a TV sitcom, dramatic series, or Hollywood movie?
- Are you making independent comedy films or movies for the Internet and want to know more about acting and directing?
- Are you writing screenplays and wish you had a better handle on comedic plot and dialogue?
- Are you auditioning for plays by your local theater group and want to strengthen your theatrical abilities?
- Do you emcee conventions, talks, or workshops and feel you don't know how to be upbeat and spontaneous in your speaking?
- Do you teach college or high school theater students and wish you could find a comedy acting book to truly inspire them?

The Art of Comedy will provide you with everything you need to know if you're eager to develop and hone your comedic talent. Learning the skills of comedy acting, such as how to improvise, create sketch characters, and perform comedy scene work, is crucial to being successful as an actor, director, screenwriter, and emcee, as well as many other professions.

If you're an actor, even a dramatic one, there are times you need to know how to think fast and talk on your feet. In today's world of Hollywood auditions, actors don't just read the scene; they have to put their own spin on it, often improvising on the spot. Many actors have a desire for fame and fortune, and sometimes want to use a quick-fix method in their approach to developing an acting career. It takes a lot of discipline to really achieve success, because there is no substitute for actually doing the work and gaining experience. Acting coach Stella Adler, who taught Marlon Brando, forbade her students to audition until they had two years of classes under their belt. When you get to an audition and really know how to break down the scene, you make a lasting impression on the casting director or producer. It can make or break a career, so why not approach it in a successful manner? Even if you land a role on a sitcom that has great writing, you're not guaranteed much of a successful career unless you have the know-how to make your character memorable and are able to work with the other actors on the set as part of a team.

If you're a writer, especially if you're writing situational or romantic comedy, you need to know different ways to make people laugh, what types of scenes evoke humor or irony, and what comedic timing is all about. Studying comedic acting will teach you those skills.

If you're a director, you need to know how to get your actors to loosen up, how to make them comfortable on the set, and how to get them to make their character genuine and authentic.

If you're a host or emcee at conferences or workshops, you need to know how to read and channel energy in your audience, as well as how to relax them, so that they will focus on your delivery.

If you're interested in stand-up and you spend time writing jokes, this book will help you open up to and work your audience much better by learning how to perceive and control energy, pacing, and timing.

If you're a teacher at the college or high school level, you need to be able to inspire your students with top-notch improvisational exercises that will train them in the world of comedy acting. This book will provide you with the exercises and lessons you need.

If you're a photographer you need to be able to direct your photo session by knowing how to loosen up your subject to get the best out of him of her.

I have designed this book to be an entire curriculum in comedy. If you were attending my comedy workshops in L.A., you would learn the same concepts and do the exact same exercises. In many ways, you have an advantage because I don't give my students a book to work from; I make them take their own notes.

Before launching into the material, let me answer some common questions people ask when they begin to study comedy acting. Some of these questions are probably on your mind, too, and even if they're not, these answers might give you some perspectives you didn't have before.

What *Exactly* Is Comedy Acting?

When I talk about comedy acting, I am referring to a performance by an actor that makes people laugh. That's not to say that comedy actors don't have other goals when performing, like making people think or change their minds about an issue, or creating situations that are both funny and bittersweet. However, in general, the hallmarks of comedy acting are humor, laughter, and a respect for the text (when there is a script).

Most people have at least a few natural comedy acting skills. As children, most of us loved telling jokes, performing physical humor, playing pranks, and making up funny stories on the fly. In junior high school, a lot of us played the class clown from time to time, driving our teachers crazy while making the rest of our classmates laugh. In high school and college, we often entertained our first loves and romantic partners with crazy antics and odd behaviors. At work, many people escape the monotony of the office environment by creating humor, in any way they can, to make their colleagues, as well as themselves, lighten up. We are all born with these types of comedy acting skills—I know that I was.

To be a successful comedy actor you must dedicate yourself by pursuing a higher level of skills and talent that take years of study to develop. As in many professions, a combination of art and science goes into transforming a person into a great comedy actor—an individual who knows precisely what to do to make people laugh and who has a broad repertoire of comedy talents. No matter how funny you were as a kid or how much laughter you can provoke at your job, becoming a skilled comedy actor takes it up several notches. It takes a lot of specialized training, along with hours and hours of practice, to truly become a successful comedic actor.

Comedy acting has a long history in the world, and has been a revered profession in many cultures. Comedic theater has existed in Western culture for thousands of years. Skilled comedic actors performed throughout the Greek, Roman, medieval, and Renaissance eras. If you've never dipped into the great masters, I suggest reading some works by funny forbearers like Aristophanes, Shakespeare, Molière, and Oscar Wilde. It can be said that these writers are truly the founders of comedy acting in that their works inspired actors to create the rudiments of comedy acting that we know today.

More recently, the birth of film and television increased the opportunities for new generations of comedy actors. The new media changed the nature of the profession in some ways, requiring comedy actors to master new skills when working in front of a camera. The worldwide popularity and expansion of film and TV has made, perhaps, the greatest contribution to comedy acting, producing scores of comedic actors who have changed the face of comedy: Charlie Chaplin, Buster Keaton, Jackie Gleason, Lucille Ball, Dick Van Dyke, Walter Matthau, Jack Lemmon, Peter Sellers, Steve Martin, Lily Tomlin, and Robin Williams—to name just a few. Let me also add the cast members of the top TV sitcoms, and, of course, the comedy sketch show that has spawned dozens of brilliant comedic actors, *Saturday Night Live*.

So, to come back to the question, what *exactly* is comedy acting? It is the ability to be completely believable in any given situation and to let the comedy come out of the situation. Being really good at it gives you the possibility to develop your personality, as well your acting skills, in ways that can offer you an amazing life and, potentially, a worldwide reputation.

What's the Difference between Comedy Acting, Improv, and Stand-up?

Comedy acting is a broad, all-encompassing term referring to a wide range of skills that an actor or artist needs in order to perform comedically. When you study comedy acting, you will be introduced to topics such as improvisation, physical comedy, sketch characters, costumes, dialects, mannerisms and gestures, facial movements, comedic timing, and a whole variety of other skills you'll need when you appear onstage.

The word *improvisation* refers to just one skill, albeit one of the most important, of comedy acting. Improv, as it is commonly called, is one of the most exciting and enjoyable, yet challenging, skills you must learn to become a well-rounded comedy actor. When improvising, you are given a circumstance or situation. It is up to you and the other actors involved in the scene to make up dialogue and action on the spot. In the best improv performances, the actors take a situation and develop it in ways that target the largest potential humor within the situation.

Stand-up comedy is yet another type of comedy. In stand-up, the comic has usually written out a script from which he or she works, with lists of jokes or anecdotes to tell. Some stand-ups don't write out their entire routine; however, they have a very good idea of topics they plan to talk about onstage. They may improvise, banter with the audience (called *riffing*), or constantly look for new perceptions and opportunities to find hilarity. Stand-ups usually work alone, but there are some well-known pairs, such as the legendary Burns and Allen, Martin and Lewis, Smothers Brothers, and Penn and Teller.

For the purposes of this book and to make things easier for you, the terms comic actor, comedy actor, and comedian will mean the same.

What Makes People Laugh?

Theories abound about what humor is and how to make people laugh. It has fascinated many great philosophers and psychologists who have written about the nature and meaning of comedy.

One could define comedy as:

a. The quality of being amusing or comical—causing laughter or amusement.

b. The ability to perceive or express what is comical or funny.

c. A state of mind or mood in a good humor.

d. A sudden unanticipated whim.

When all is said and done, we cannot truly say there is a rock-solid, universally accepted understanding of the human funny bone. It seems that anything is possible and that every new comedic actor has a chance to redefine the nature of comedy. Think, for example, how the modern age has ranged from comedy greats such as Charlie Chaplin and Buster Keaton starring in silent films, to TV sitcom legends Lucille Ball and Jackie Gleason, to today's comics. They each have their own style—and no two are exactly alike.

The only truth that seems to exist is that comic actors can make people laugh in a thousand different ways. They can talk funny by speaking fast, slow, with an accent, or at a speed that people find weird and unique; they can mimic people by exaggerating mannerisms and gestures; they can use their body to create humor by falling down, stumbling, or stretching their limbs in unnatural ways. They can create characters who are strange, warped, or have mental or physical oddities; act stupid or smart; or recite stories, jokes, or lines that get the audience to expect one thing, but then be surprised by another. The reversal of expectations is often cited as the foundational theory of comedy. You can explore all of these when studying comedy acting and seeking to define your own style.

As long as we're talking about *what* makes people laugh, let me throw in the related issue: *why* do people laugh? Again, theories abound on why laughing is a human trait, such as that laughter releases endorphins that are healthy for the body or that laughter is a type of emotional release. There is even evidence that laughter greatly helps the body and serves as a remedy to illness. I happen to believe that laughter moves energy around in our bodies. We laugh because our body is filled with energy, and if that energy doesn't move around, we can become dull and unhealthy. This is why I feel that to do comedy, you must learn to become free and to let your energy flow freely. Just as an athlete needs to stretch and become flexible, you need to stretch and become comedically flexible. Consider this book as your very own Pilates workout of comedy.

What If I Don't Think I'm Very Funny?

For some, it's likely that people may have told you, "You're really funny! You should do comedy." If that's so, great! I'm sure feedback like this from people in your life inspires you to believe in your comedic talents. But some of you may not believe you are naturally funny and may be worried about whether or not you can do it. I would guess that you are attracted to comedy because you like to laugh, but may feel shy about being funny or when making attempts to be funny, as no one laughs.

Don't worry about it. No matter how many people have or have not told you that you are funny, it simply doesn't matter. What counts is your own attitude toward yourself. As I tell all of my students, once you begin thinking you are funny, you will be. I don't think God created anyone on this planet thinking, "You, over there, here's two arms, two legs, and a brain, but sorry, I'm making you one of the not-funny ones."

I've had students who were shy and inhibited blossom into working comedy actors once they began believing in themselves. If your instinct told you to read this book, it means you want to be funnier. You could have purchased another book, but given that you picked up this one, it clearly reveals a wish to explore your sense of humor and learn to make others laugh. Something inside you is calling you to become more playful, more joyful, and more creative. You want to expand your funny bone, your personality, or move through inhibitions and issues that are holding you back. So, if that's the case, stop thinking you are not funny! Maybe you're just a late bloomer.

How Do I Find the Funny in Me?

Finding the funny in you is a matter of discovering yourself. Each one of us has our own unique style and brand of comedy—because comedy arises from inside. Each one of us is different, and that's why the world has a Jerry Seinfeld, a Whoopi Goldberg, a Billy Crystal, a Rosie O'Donnell, a Chris Rock, a Paula Poundstone, a Steven Wright, a Roseanne, a Dave Chappelle, an Ellen DeGeneres, a Jamie Foxx, a Sarah Silverman, and lots of other funny individuals, each with his or her own distinctive style.

I believe that every comedy actor has his or her own *comedic core.* Your comedic core is your own sense of comedy that arises from your childhood, family, and life experiences—everything that amuses you and that you can bring to other people to make them laugh.

In my philosophy, the process of finding your comedic core is like peeling an onion. Deep inside each of us is a sweet, juicy, innocent core, but over the years we've added a bunch of additional layers to protect us. As a result, when you study comedy acting, you need to open and peel back the layers, one by one, to reveal your playful, funny core.

What becomes fascinating is that all the extra layers you peel back are actually your life experiences. Whatever recipe you are creating, you can use all those layers of onion as ingredients in your comedy. Talking about your family, friends, and life is the best source of your comedy. When you talk about yourself, it opens up a huge arena of material from which you can pull and build upon. That's why each of us is different and needs to mine our comedy gold. Compare, for example, the comedy of someone like Steven Wright, who created a comedic character whose personality seems completely deadpan and serious, to the comedy of someone like Robin Williams, whose comedy is a non-stop train of thought.

Another point I need to make about finding the comedy in you is that the more authentic and truthful your comedy is, the funnier it will be. I have people who come to my workshops and create very odd and strange sketch characters that are simply not funny. What's missing usually is that their character is not truthful, and the audience can detect something is missing. The actors are trying too hard to make us laugh, but the real humor arises from letting us see the reality of that person. Rather than *pushing* comedy, I believe that you have to *allow* it to happen.

I teach people how to become completely believable in whatever they create, and to let the comedy grow out of the reality of the situation. You do not have to try to *make* the scene funny to create comedy. There must be some grain of truth before anything funny can take place.

A good example of this is the legendary television show, *I Love Lucy*. Decades after its creation, the program continues to delight new audiences every day, because Lucy and Desi didn't play their scenes for laughs, but for real, allowing the humor to emerge from their predicaments. Once the reality of a situation has been established, the actors can use their comedy imaginations to bring out the magic that continuously makes the world laugh.

Does My Age Matter?

No. Your age doesn't matter one iota when it comes to learning comedy. At any age you can learn comedy acting and develop performance skills to use in your life or turn into a career. In fact, having lots of life experiences with funny situations can be very useful in creating comedy, so the older you are, the more it might even be to your advantage.

There is a student in my class named Marion Gibbons, who is eighty-three years *young*. I met Marion when she appeared as a guest on the "Senior Inspiration" segment I taped for my TV show *Feel Good TV with Paul Ryan & Friends*. In the segment, I interviewed Marion because she is the president of the Hollywood Heritage Museum, and she was a great interviewee. We talked afterward and she became interested in studying comedy with me. With her husband and children already deceased, Marion wanted to keep herself busy by learning new things, rather than waste the rest of her life away. So she enrolled in my comedy classes. After about nine months, she started booking commercials left, right, and center. Feeling younger, she's become friends with several of the younger actors in the class. How's that for an eighty-three-year-old woman?

On the opposite side of the spectrum, I coach a great young kid named William May, who just turned thirteen. He was originally born in Argentina. He and his family moved to Miami and now live in Los Angeles. William began singing and dancing a few years ago, and his dad Donald wanted him to learn comedy, so I began coaching him. His father then asked me to write a stand-up act for William, and I did—and he's already booked two shows. William emcees many events in Los Angeles using his stand-up comedy act.

In the end, your age has no effect on your enjoyment or your possible success in studying comedy acting. What matters most is that you are willing to go outside your comfort zone in order to be free to experiment and peel your onion.

No matter what age you are, this book can bring you a new freedom and a new career. You too can be like Marion or William and may soon discover the proverbial fountain of youth in your own comedy.

Do My Looks or My Voice Matter?

Again, the answer is *no*. What's amazing about achieving success on any level in comedy acting—whether it's in your local amateur class or in a Hollywood audition—is that whatever you think might be a fault or blemish in your appearance, or a physical trait you are not proud of, can be turned into an advantage. In fact, some of the funniest students in my class are those who are willing to use their appearances or voices for humor, often by making fun of themselves in a self-deprecating way.

I call things like appearance and voice your *isms*, and I tell my students to use them, because these qualities are what make you unique. Your *isms* set you apart from other actors and contribute to making you more memorable than the next person in an audition. You don't need matinee idol looks to make it into TV, film, or theater. Sure, some people in Hollywood place an emphasis on youth and beauty, but TV is full of stars that have unique *isms*. Some examples have been Fran Drescher and her heavily accented Brooklyn accent; Roseanne Barr with her short, chunky body and whiney voice; heavyset John Candy; and three Seinfeld regulars: Jason Alexander, with his short, everyman look; Michael Richards, with his lanky and loose body; and Julia Louis-Dreyfus, with her normal-looking appearance. None of these actors had stereotypical looks of superstardom, yet they all made it very big.

Normal looks can even be useful in comedy because agents and casting directors (and eventually the viewers) can relate more to a "normal" person than to someone with a super good appearance. Blemishes, unusual physical looks, and quirky voices can also be the starting point of characters you build and develop to use in your comedy sketches. Some of the greatest comedic characters from *Saturday Night Live* were based on funny voices or physical characteristics, such as Dana Carvey's "Church Lady" character and Chris Kattan's "Mango" character.

In the end, what really counts when becoming a successful comedy actor is your degree of confidence and self-respect and the skills you bring to the table. You can have the most attractive face and body the world has ever seen, but if you don't believe in yourself and haven't worked on your talent, then the powers that control the gates to stardom are unlikely to show much interest in furthering your career.

One final comment on appearance: It is also beneficial to be honest and forthright about your appearance when submitting headshots for auditions. You don't want to send photos that are so touched up that when you arrive at the audition the casting people say, "You don't look at all like your picture!"

Why Learn Comedy if I'm a Dramatic Actor?

If you are a dramatic actor I can tell you without a doubt that studying comedic acting will help you for many reasons. And I know, because I've trained many dramatic actors.

Even if a movie is a drama without a single funny line of dialogue within fifty miles of the screenplay, the actor who has studied comedy acting can gain an edge over the other actors. A comedy actor develops many vital acting skills due to training in improv, comedic timing, and sketch character creation. These skills will improve your dramatic acting and help you work more closely with the other actors on the set. Dramatic actors have told me that their dramatic work has greatly improved since they studied comedy because they feel more free and less predictable in front of the camera. They also have confidence in their ability to adapt and change, are not intimidated to be in front of countless people, and feel completely uninhibited to say or do anything that may help develop a character.

Can I Make Money from My Comedy?

Does ice cream melt if you leave it in the sun? Will a hungry dog steal a steak left on the counter? Would you accept a Mercedes Benz if I offered it to you for free?

In other words, duh, of course. You can make lots of money if you learn how to make people laugh and are committed to using your comedic talents wisely.

If you want to catch the brass ring, you'll want to come to Hollywood to study further and audition for comedy roles in TV and film. Each year, thousands of kids and adults arrive in Los Angeles seeking their opportunity to attract an agent and audition for one of hundreds of TV sitcom pilots being cast. You can become part of this crowd, and if you use this book and practice what you learn, you will actually boost your chances. I needn't tell you that some of the most successful, highest-paid performers in the world today are the comedy actors who star in long-running TV sitcoms. Who wouldn't have loved to be one of the stars of *Seinfeld* or *Friends*?

And there are dozens of other ways you can earn money using what you will learn in this book. As I said in the beginning of this chapter, you can make independent comedies, short movies for the Internet, write a screenplay, or become a host of a local cable TV show. There are also a myriad of ways to use your comedy acting skills in the world of business by being able to loosen up and lighten up your communication skills.

By the way, if you come to Hollywood some day, and you do make it, please give my book credit for helping you get started. I'm open and available for inclusion in all Oscar, Tony, and Emmy acceptance speeches. You can keep the statue, as long as you give me the credit (well, a chauffeured limo to the event would be great, too—and a house in Italy wouldn't be bad, now that I think of it, but if all else fails, I'm a 38 regular).

Using This Book

I recommend that you read the book in sequential order, rather than skip around. The chapters are organized in a specific sequence from easier activities to more challenging ones. Learning to do comedy requires building skills progressively, so you'll fare much better if you follow the order I've established. The even-numbered chapters contain exercises, and the odd-numbered chapters explain the concepts and ideas for the exercises.

Learning comedy takes time, so be patient with yourself and with others who may be working with you if you are conducting or participating in a workshop. In our quick-fix society, people expect to have immediate results, but with comedy, you have to be willing to pay your dues through repetition. Remember, it takes time to learn a skill to the point of mastery. In the old days of vaudeville, the great actors of comedy and burlesque did eight shows a week, if not eight shows a day. They lived and breathed comedy and they learned it by *doing* it.

Coming back to my peeling the onion analogy, you need to peel the onion to find your comedic core—and that takes time because you may have a lot of layers to remove. The amount of time it will take depends on where you are starting. One girl I taught, Jean Black, was terribly shy and uptight, but within a year and half she created five very clever characters and performed a one-woman show. I've also had people who moved quickly through my classes, unlocking their comedy in as few as six months. I can't predict your timeline, but whatever it is, it will unfold naturally for you—so don't rush it.

Below is an overview of what we are going to cover:

IMPROV

You will explore dozens of improvisations that you can perform with other people. While all improvs teach you something about how to think fast and create your own dialogue out of thin air, many of them have other goals, such as teaching you to listen, to work closely with other actors, to use dialects, to become uninhibited and free, and to use props. Improv is one of the fundamental skills of comedy acting, and this book will give you abundant opportunities to practice and hone your skills.

DEVELOPING A SKETCH COMEDY CHARACTER

Sketch comedy character work refers to creating a character that you will use in your performance. Think of the many great sketch comedy characters that have left their mark in the world of comedy: Lily Tomlin's "Edith Anne" and "Ernestine" (the telephone operator); Mike Myers's "Austin Powers"; or Eddie Murphy's characters in the movie *The Klumps.*

You'll learn how to find characters you can imitate and develop. You'll find ways to look within to identify opportunities for sketch characters from your own life or from your own private world. Robin Williams grew up as an only child and imagined dozens of characters, which now appear in his routines. You'll also discover how to look at your family and the people you see on the street to figure out how to portray them and exaggerate their traits. Many sketch characters are built by copying the mannerisms and behavior of people all around us. For example, Mike Myers based his "Coffee Talk" lady on his former mother-in-law. You'll learn to use props, wigs, and costumes to allow you to move outside of yourself to portray others.

Sketch comedy character work is one of the best ways to stretch your talents. Even if you never use a character you invent, the character resides within you and can inspire you to create other characters later.

COMEDIC TIMING

One of the important skills you will learn from this book is how to develop an advanced sense of comedic timing, which includes knowing when to recommence after the audience has started laughing. There is a particular timing for this, and if you get it wrong, you will ruin the joke or unwittingly tell the audience you want them to stop laughing. You learn comedic timing only by doing it, and the improvs and other exercises contained in this book will give you the chance to master this skill—as long as you do them in front of others.

COMEDY CHARACTER DEVELOPMENT

Comedy character development is a necessity when you land a part in a play, film, or TV show. Although a writer has created your character, it remains one-dimensional unless you can bring it to life. Scripts never tell the actor everything he or she needs to know about the character. It's up to *you* to go beyond the script. To do so, you need to know how to explore your character and extract the most comedy you can get out of it.

Character comedy development is particularly important for TV sitcoms, because the actor who portrays the character can affect the script and put his or her own spin on the direction of the character. For example, on the TV sitcom *Will & Grace*, it became clear that Sean Hayes, who portrayed the character Jack, was brilliant at physical comedy, so the writers used that when writing scenes for his character.

You'll learn how to recognize your strengths as a comedy actor so you, too, can add your own flavor to a character that has already been scripted.

COMEDY SCENE WORK

Every comedy scene has an embedded truth that the actors must uncover. Call it the pot of gold or the heart of the scene, but if the actors miss the truth, the scene loses its believability.

I've created a technique that allows you to evaluate a scene and figure out its truth. You'll be able to understand why it's humorous, and more importantly, how you can personalize the scene to make it funnier.

COMEDIC FREEDOM

One of the most important results of your work will be learning how to achieve comedic freedom. As I said earlier, comedy is all about freedom. It's about being able to use your mind and body without any constraints or inhibitions. Similar to the freedom that a martial artist exhibits when kicking or the freedom an athlete feels when running with complete abandonment, comedy freedom is a state of mind that allows you to be funny without any limits. Something takes over your mind and body, and you enter into a natural state of flow. You stop analyzing what you are doing and worrying about what other people are thinking. Many sides of your brain are working at the same time—all in the service of your comedy.

This book will help you achieve comedic freedom by offering you great exercises for you to practice your craft. In many of the exercises I've included dozens of options so that you can perform them over and over again in endless variations. As you will discover, it is the repetition that slowly releases you and leads you to your freedom.

I encourage you to do all these exercises as many times as you can. The more you do them, the freer you will get. Through practice and experimentation, your comedy imagination will stretch, and you'll naturally develop funnier and deeper comedy characters and scenes.

AUDITIONING TECHNIQUES

I've had many directors tell me that actors today don't seem to look their fellow actors in the eye during the audition process. When you study improv, you learn how to do this, because comedy acting requires all the actors to react to each other—and a lot of comedy comes from the looks you give your partners.

I've also spoken to many casting directors who told me that many actors come to read a script and do not truly understand what the scene requires from them. A foundation in comedy acting techniques will help you learn how to analyze a scene in order to find the character's humor, a skill that you can bring into any dramatic work. I work with a lot of actors on this skill, and I constantly tell them, "Don't memorize the script. Keep reading it over until you completely understand what's going on. The writer is writing about something in life, and your job, as an actor, is to understand the writer's message. Once you find the message, you need to personalize it and give it your own spin." This is what casting directors are *really* looking for.

Related to this is the fact that these days many casting directors will ask the actors to improvise the script. A director might say, "I like what you did, but I'd like you to improvise for me and see what you can come up with." One reason casting directors do this is to see if the actor can think of something the writer may not have. Directors like Woody Allen routinely have their actors improvise. Mr. Allen is known to give an actor the script right before he shoots, because he intentionally wants an improvisational feel to the scene. Mr. Allen relies heavily on casting the right actor and trusts that the actor will provide what he is looking for. Director Robert Altman also strove for dialogue that had a lot of overlapping conversation and used a lot of improv to achieve this effect.

Learning to become a great comedy actor is pointless unless you know how to show your talents off in front of the powers that make the decisions to hire you or not. That's why I've included tons of valuable, practical tips about auditioning and casting that I've learned through my more than twenty-five years of experience in Hollywood. We'll discuss key issues like:

How to Bring Energy into an Audition

A lot of auditions begin with what seems to be lighthearted schmoozing, but what's really going on is that the casting people are checking you out and trying to test your personality. I'll show you how to be "on" from the moment you enter the room, so they can feel your vibe, freedom, and energy.

How to Read It Right the First Time

It used to be that casting directors would give you two or three takes in an audition to nail your scene, but not anymore. I'll teach you how to work your way up to the level of freedom and energy you need on the very first read. It doesn't matter if you were great in the car on the way to the audition; it's what you do with the few minutes you have in the audition room that counts.

How to Personalize the Scene

As I discussed, a lot of actors when auditioning rely strictly on the dialogue in the script for the humor. This won't cut it if you can't figure out how to make the scene *yours*. I will teach you how to understand the scene, figure out why it is funny, personalize it so you'll have an emotional connection from your own life, and then know what your character is trying to do in the scene. You'll see how to find nuances in a scene so that your audition stands out, going beyond what the writer may have thought about. A quick example: When I auditioned for the movie *Charlie Chan and the Curse of the Dragon Queen*, I read the script and saw that my character, the assistant to a wacky police chief, happened to be a hypochondriac. I decided that I would exaggerate this character trait. So, before my audition I bought a thermometer, a blood pressure kit, a large pillbox, and some other items that would relate to a hypochondriac and brought them to the audition. The director absolutely loved my use of props, and fortunately I got the part.

How to Have Confidence in Yourself

Auditioning requires a large degree of confidence and belief in your self. The more effort you put in prior to your audition, the more confident you will be when you walk into the room. Also I highly recommend doing some inner work on yourself, so that you shed some of the baggage you might be carrying around from the past. The more confident we are with ourselves, the more confident we can be in front of others. I'll show you some other approaches, such as industry networking and show business research you can use to maintain your confidence in front of important people who may hold the key to your future.

Diving into the Comedy Pool

As you read and practice the concepts and principles of comedy, I invite you to dive into the comedy pool and get yourself fully wet. Get involved in comedy in as many ways as you can. Here are some suggestions to check out now or anytime you can.

HANG OUT WITH FUNNY PEOPLE

The late Leonard Spiegelgass, one of the top comedy writers of his time, once told me, "You want to be a ball player, hang out in the ballpark." So I say to you, "You want to do comedy, hang out with funny people." Just as with tennis, if you want to better your game, you need to play with people better than you. Seek out people who love talking, bantering, telling jokes, and especially those who do comedy acting for a living. If you can find yourself a mentor, so much the better.

HANG OUT WITH DIFFERENT PEOPLE

Befriend many types of people and add diversity to your life. Different people can help you learn things about characters and dialects, which you can work into your comedy. If you are sixteen, hang out with people of other ages. Find people who have some character to them. Older people have often formed character traits that can be quite amusing. Talk to a veteran waitress, for example. They possess unique character traits and often have an outrageousness quality to them. As Sir Michael Caine once said, "You can learn so much just by watching people in subways, buses, planes, and trains."

READ AND STUDY COMEDY LEGENDS

Get to know legendary comedy actors. You can learn so much from the various paths that actors have taken. Read biographies, or research comedy legends who have inspired you. Visit the Academy of Motion Pictures Arts and Sciences Library if you're visiting Los Angeles. Access articles and biographies on comedy actors, directors, writers, and producers from the past and present on the Internet. Watch television shows from the past and present at the Museum of TV & Radio, located in Beverly Hills, California, and New York City.

READ COMEDY SCRIPTS

Buy scripts from movies and TV shows and read them to beef up your knowledge. Neil Simon, perhaps our greatest American comedy playwright, will teach you how to construct a comedy scene with a beginning, middle, and end and how to create an arc in the emotional movement of the characters. He will also teach you how to find the truth in a scene. His writing is so precise that an actor must act the dialogue *exactly* as written to perfect the comedy timing.

STUDY AND WATCH YOURSELF

I highly recommend that you videotape yourself and study your comedy work. Don't be vain. Tape yourself from many different angles so that you become comfortable on camera and are able to assess which are your best angles.

DON'T BE AFRAID TO TAKE RISKS AND MAKE MISTAKES

Taking chances, even if you fail, is vital to learning comedy. It is truly a gift when you can fall on your butt within an atmosphere of learning and growth. My studies at Los Angeles City College gave me the opportunity to perform badly, for which I am most grateful. At the end of my first semester, I performed a scene from *The Ginger Man*, by J. P. Donleavy, which is a very intense play. My college classmate Kerry Holden and I emoted, slapped each other, threw theatrical blocks across the stage, and acted larger-than-life. We both thought we had channeled Elizabeth Taylor and Richard Burton from the movie *Who's Afraid of Virginia Woolf?* We knew we had been brilliant. We were shocked when we received a D for the scene! Today, I know that failures like this helped me grow enormously. Give yourself the freedom to take risks and make mistakes.

TRUST YOUR INSTINCTS

I believe that how you personally feel about your work is just as important, if not more, than what anyone else can tell you. This is especially true if you find yourself learning from a highly critical coach. In my classroom I am firm, but I prefer to nurture my students. I know some acting coaches and teachers think there is great value in being tough on their students. Ultimately, trust your own instincts. If a coach tells you that you'll never make it, don't fall into the trap of thinking that person has the last word on your career. Remember: the list of successful performers who were once told that they "would never make it" is long; their names could fill pages and pages. So believe in yourself!

DO THE WORK

As I said, comedy acting takes lots of practice, so jump right into the work. Don't procrastinate. Hopefully, if you're like most of my students, once you start you will find yourself quickly becoming addicted to comedy. Yes, it can be difficult and scary at first, but dive in. You deserve to give yourself the opportunity to play, have more joy, and be something other than who you are. Laughing is a great prescription for a healthier life—don't deprive yourself of the opportunity.

Starting a Comedy Workshop

I've written this book to be a complete comedy workshop, and I hope you will find a group of people to work with and to take advantage of my teaching methods.

Starting a comedy workshop is not difficult at all. If you're an actor, you probably know at least a few actors who can benefit from this book. Call them up and invite them to join you on a weekly basis. I would venture to guess that within a few weeks your group will double in size, as more people find out about your comedy workshop group.

If you're a college student, you'll probably have no trouble finding other students to join a comedy group at your school.

If you're working at a job and hoping to transition your career into stand-up or professional comedy, you could place some bulletins around the office to advertise a comedy get-together during lunchtime or after work. Performing comedy at lunch is a wonderful way to reenergize yourself and colleagues.

You could start your own comedy workshop in your neighborhood or place of worship. Use your home or rent a workspace.

No matter where you are, all you need is a minimum of two to five people to get your workshop going, although having seven to ten people adds humor and energy to the comedy. The more people, the merrier, because having an audience around to laugh always makes things funnier. You'll notice that the workshop participants will become more humorous and will take bigger risks when there's an audience watching them. We're all hams, after all.

Try to get a wide range of people of different ages and ethnicities. Diversity helps the comedy.

Once your group has practiced for perhaps six months and you've developed various skits and characters, why not host a comedy showcase? Give your workshop members a chance to perform in front of others and gain experience. Charge money and make a profit. Become successful at it.

Comedy Can Help Your Personal Life

Comedy can make you more interesting. In the dating world, humor is vital—Internet dating sites are full of singles looking for people with senses of humor. When all is said and done, what sustains many relationships is, in fact, a sense of humor. Do you want to be with someone who is spontaneous or with someone who's as dull as a cardboard box?

There are those who say people who are either very pretty or very wealthy can be boring as hell. They have not fully developed their personality or developed a sense of humor because they've relied on the looks or the money. Comedy enriches your communication skills.

Comedy Affects Any Job

Studying comedy acting can have a significant impact on many jobs and careers, too. As I mentioned earlier, writers can benefit from comedy and improv classes that spark creativity and that help them become more articulate and flexible.

I occasionally have business people in my classes, and they tell me that comedy acting has positively affected their work. They say my classes have taught them to be much more verbally flexible, to look people directly in the eyes, to have the guts to say what they really mean, and to be quick on their feet in meetings. Also, given that the daily grind of work can become tedious at times, comedy can bring a new level of joy that simply cannot be found in the workplace.

How Does the Paul Ryan Comedy Method Compare to Others?

Some comedy books provide many improv exercises but do not contain a core of information, philosophy, and advice. My method is geared toward training the entire actor. The exercises in this book will help you build a comedy arsenal so that you can think clearly when a director says, "Can you show me what you can add to this scene?" You'll learn how to set you and your acting partner up for success in improvisational work and how improv will help your timing greatly with scripted scenes.

It is my joy to bring you what I have been doing for the past twenty years: unlocking the keys to one's comedy vault. To succeed in comedy, as in any other endeavor, you have to pay your dues. Comedy is something you cannot talk about; you have to *do it*. In my classes, all the students work three or four times per three-hour class. My job is to open the floodgates and create a safe, supportive environment where my students can unfold their talent. As someone who considers himself a spiritual person, I feel nurturing a student I'm coaching is essential to my work.

LEVEL I: BEGINNING COMEDY EXERCISES

OKAY, IT'S TIME TO LET THE COMEDY GAMES BEGIN. I'M SURE you're eager to begin *doing* comedy, because as I've said before, there's no substitute for "the doing." Just as you won't build biceps without exercise, you won't start being funny unless you get up on your feet and get the ball rolling.

In this chapter I'm going to introduce the following four fundamental groups of comedy acting exercises. They are the foundation for all the skills you will master in any type of comedy you may do.

- Building energy
- Honing your listening skills
- Releasing inhibitions
- Expanding your possibilities

You'll find no better way to learn these four skills than by performing the various exercises in this chapter. Comedy exercises help stretch your comedy muscles and loosen up your mind, body, and mouth. You'll learn how to work with other comedy actors and to play off whatever they say or do while on the stage or set. Consider these exercises as your initiation into the magic of comedy acting. If you can do these while having fun and creating laughter, you're well on your way.

For each of the four groups you'll have two to five individual exercises. I created most of these routines from scratch, experimenting and perfecting them over the years. My classes have spent countless, hilarious hours training with these exercises, which I'm sure you will find just as fun, too.

Most of the exercises require a minimum of two to three people, although a larger group is always better. Working with others builds teamwork, humor, and effectiveness. Diversity gives the group more possibilities for successful comedy because of the different backgrounds and experiences. Also, as anyone with a sense of humor knows, having an audience listen and laugh drives most actors to take bigger risks and become funnier. Working with a laughing audience will also teach you comedic timing, which I'll talk about later in this chapter. So try to put together as large a group as you can.

You don't need to do every single exercise in each group (except the warm-up exercises, which you should do every single time). You can pick and choose individual exercises from each group as you wish, or vary them from session to session. Your choice of exercise might depend on how many people you have, who likes which exercise, or who's running the show.

Guidelines for Workshop Participants

If you create a workshop or participate in one led by someone else, I highly recommend that you adopt some guidelines and ask all participants to follow them. They don't need to be elaborate; a simple set of rules concerning the operation of the workshop puts everyone on the same page. Most important, having guidelines creates a feeling of emotional safety for the participants. Keep in mind that you are conducting a creative process, and that creative space must be protected.

1. Out of respect to fellow actors, when you have a workshop, do not enter or exit during an actual scene or critique.

2. When people are working, please do not participate in side conversations or whisper, as it takes the focus away from those working.

3. If you have a schedule, please stick to it. When people arrive late or don't show up, it undermines the integrity of the group.

4. Please make an attempt to see comedy plays, films and videos, as well as reading comedy plays and scripts, which you can find on line. (www.scripts.com is one option)

5. Change your attire periodically when getting together. Allow yourself to be as creative as possible and sometimes wearing different clothes does help.

6. Camaraderie with your fellow students is vital. Observing the work of others is very important and facilitates your growth as well.

7. Please be aware of your physicality. I encourage physical freedom, but be aware of causing any uncomfortable physicality with your fellow actors. This is acting; don't hurt each other, folks.

8. You must honor complete confidentially at all times. Whatever happens in improv, stays in improv.

9. Please do not say anything negative to your fellow actors regarding their physicality, race, religion, or creed.

10. Enjoy yourself. This is comedy, not root canal.

Warm-Up Exercises

Before initiating any comedy acting work, I always ask my students to do a set of warm-up exercises to charge up their mind and body. It's a bit more difficult to be funny without warming up. These warm-ups should be done at the start of each and every time your group gathers to work. Don't overlook them, as they will make a huge difference in the rest of your time together. (Don't be surprised if you see me looking in your window to make sure you are doing them!)

GENERAL WARM-UP

One of the signature exercises I created and use whenever I host an event or teach a class is to ask people to stand up and go through what I call "I'm Letting Go!" This exercise helps everyone release tension, stress, and that mind-numbing chatter in their heads. It may sound corny to you at first, but you'll be amazed at the energy, smiles, and positive vibes it brings to an entire audience or group of students. I have never seen this exercise fail to get people into the present moment and to feel more alive and ready to work.

Begin by standing up tall, like a Dallas Cowboys cheerleader, and shout each of the following two phrases three times along with the accompanying movements.

1. Bring your right arm to your left shoulder and move it up to the sky and shout "I'm!"

2. Bring your left arm to your right shoulder and then up to the sky as you shout "Letting!"

3. Raise both arms into a V formation to the sky and shout "Go!"

4. Do the above three times.

5. Next, use the same arm movements from steps 1–3, but use the words "I Feel Great!" instead, with one movement per word.

BODY WARM-UP

These warm-up exercises loosen your body and release tension that all of us tend to carry in our neck, shoulders, and everywhere else in the body.

1. Begin by letting your head fall forward. Rest your chin on the top of your sternum. Roll your head back three times to the right and then three times to the left.

2. Do three shoulder circles in a backward motion, followed by three shoulder circles in a forward motion.

3. Bring your legs together and stand up straight. Raise your shoulders upward, as if you are shrugging, and then push them back and then down. Get your body into a good neutral standing position, so that you feel everything is in alignment.

4. Spread your legs, hip width apart, and bend over, leading with your head, shoulders, and upper chest. Keep your legs straight as you bend over. Let your upper shoulders and head become heavy without forcing the bend. Continue to slowly bend forward to the ground until your fingers touch the floor—or as far as you can go. You'll become more flexible over time, so don't strain to touch the floor if you are unable.

5. While bent over, release your knees by bending them. Your body should be hanging, like a Raggedy Ann doll, toward the floor. Shake and release any tension, leaving all negativity on the floor.

6. Finally, come back up very slowly, one vertebra at a time, using your stomach muscles. When you are standing, shake your body and throw off any remaining tension.

FACIAL MUSCLES WARM-UP

You now need to get your facial muscles and mouth loosened up, so that your face is pliable and free of tension. Do the series of movements below three times in a row. They will help wake up the mouth muscles, which will greatly help your enunciation and articulation. Let Jim Carrey's flexible face be your inspiration.

1. Massage your jaw muscles all around your mouth and cheeks with your fingers. As you rub the jaw muscles, pretend you are Olga or Hans from Sweden, and slowly say "Yah, yah, yah" three times.

2. Next, pout your lips forward in an exaggerated fashion, as if you were a baboon, and say "Ooh."

3. Now, open your mouth as wide as possible and say "Aah." Close your mouth while saying "Mmmm."

BREATH AND VOICE WARM-UPS

The following three exercises work on your breathing and voice. Loud, clear vocalization is also crucial when you're doing comedy and improv in TV, film, or stage. You need to speak up with good tonality so that every member of the audience can hear you.

The key is to get your voice to come from a deep region within you, because it connects you to your feelings and makes your voice sound richer and more expressive. If your voice comes from your throat area, it makes you sound as if you are disconnected from your feelings. As an actor, it is *vital* to incorporate your feelings into your work. You have to get energy flowing and moving throughout you at all times. If the audience doesn't feel and hear you, your work will become null and void.

Let me also point out that most TV sitcoms today are filmed with three cameras in front of a live audience. If you don't have energy or cannot be heard, you'll be toast before you can say Jennifer Aniston. If you perform comedy on a stage, the producer or director may sit in the back of the theater in the very last seat to test you. If they can't hear you, you'll be back out on the street. That's why I encourage you to commit 100 percent to these exercises to open your energy and get your voice built up. I suggest you do at least five to ten minutes of breathing and vocal warm-ups before you start any improv or sketch work. As I tell my students all the time, how well you do in the audition process depends entirely on how well you've mastered your daily preparation work.

DEEP BREATHING

Breathing is the key to your energy and life force. As an actor, having good control of your breathing is vital. When you feel stressed, your breath becomes shallow and your entire body suffers.

1. Place your hands on your stomach and open your mouth so that it's comfortably loose.

2. Slowly and deeply breathe in through your mouth, making an audible inhalation sound. Let your stomach, back, and lungs fill up with air. Do not raise your chest or shoulders. Hold this breath for a second and then breathe out, slowly pulling your stomach in and letting the air come out of your mouth. Do this at least three times.

3. On the fourth breath, let out a nice deep "Ah" from deep within you as you exhale. Focus on letting your voice come from your groin area, not from your throat. Do this at least three times.

DEEPENING AND ANCHORING YOUR VOICE

This exercise builds your vocal strength by expanding your lung capacity. You will find that your voice will be lower and more powerful, as it comes from a much deeper place.

1. Lie on your back and relax. Look upward.

2. Breathe in through your mouth, keeping it wide open and allowing an inhalation sound to escape. Fill your stomach, ribs, and back with air.

3. On a full inhalation, slowly let the air out through your mouth, leaving it open as your stomach muscles retract. Do this three times.

4. Inhale again. On the exhalation, release an "Ah" sound as slowly as possible. Do this three times.

ARTICULATING WITH VOWELS AND CONSONANTS

This exercise will help you learn to enunciate and move your mouth muscles. It's also mildly amusing to watch a group of people do this.

1. Open your mouth as wide as possible and say the long and short vowel sounds. Use the following as a visual aid:

Long	Short
A [as in *a*ce]	**ah** [as in b*a*t]
E [as in *e*ven]	**eh** [as in p*e*t]
I [as in *i*ce]	**ih** [as in *i*t]
O [as in *o*pen]	**oo** [as is p*oo*p]
U [as in *u*se]	**uh** [as in *u*p]

2. Now pronounce all the consonants except X from deep within your belly. Also, let your stomach muscles go in and out.

Buh	Cuh	Duh	Fuh	Guh	Huh	Juh	Kuh
Luh	Muh	Nuh	Puh	Quh	Ruh	Suh	Tuh
Vuh	Wuh	Yuh	Zuh				

3. Repeat "Huh" several times at the end, to really feel your stomach muscles go in and out. Remember, if your stomach muscles are not engaged when you're talking, you're missing the emotional and vocal connection.

The Fundamental Group Exercises

Now that we're warmed up, it's time to start the exercises in the four fundamental groups of comedy acting. Remember, these groups are the foundation for all the skills you will master in any type of comedy you may perform. As I mentioned, you don't have to do every single exercise in each group, but pick and choose from each one and vary them in your sessions.

GROUP 1 EXERCISES: BUILDING ENERGY

I'm sure you've seen at least one stage play in which the actors were lagging, dragging, and sagging, and you thought to yourself, "I gotta get out of here, this is dullsville." Well, comedy is the same—it demands large amounts of energy. Without it, your audience will be in a different zip code.

Creating energy involves being 100 percent committed to what you are doing onstage and focusing your mind and body on your role. Many actors call it "Being On," which is a frame of mind and attitude that changes your body when you put yourself in this state. You're like an athlete in the middle of a championship game, or a concert violinist playing a solo in front of five thousand people, or, come to think of it, an actor onstage.

Your attitude greatly affects your energy. As soon as you are selected to do a scene, it helps to be positive and confident that you are about to do solid work. Don't let anxiety about what you're supposed to say or do take over your mind. Stay cool, calm, collected, and in control of your craft.

Energy requires focus. You cannot allow any distractions in your mind as you play out your scene. The minute your mind wanders, and you think about your socks falling down or how you left the coffee pot on at home, your creativity falters.

THE ALLITERATION REPETITION

This is the best exercise to help you develop energy while performing improv. It is based on a vaudeville high-energy technique called *alliteration*.

This is a great exercise to repeat as many times as you can. I've provided many variations that will help you.

PEOPLE NEEDED: 2

SCENE: Two strangers meet at a bus stop, an airport, a train depot, or any common travel location.

DIRECTIONS: Place two chairs together on the stage area. One actor is seated, looking out at the traffic going by. (The actor should try to see the traffic in his or her mind.) The second actor enters from the side with a sense of urgency and a strong intention to communicate with the seated stranger. The two introduce themselves to each other and ask each other what they do for a living, using one of the alliterative four-worded professions listed on pages 10–11. They continue chatting, constantly repeating what the other said, slightly changing it only to make the conversation move forward.

Keep your responses brief and your sentences short. This is a comedy rhythm exercise, almost like a verbal ping-pong match at high speed, which is accomplished by constantly playing off each other. The key is to immediately repeat 75 percent of the conversation back to the other actor. The remaining 25 percent of the conversation should focus on continuing the verbal exchange so that it seems like a real conversation. Don't think; just repeat, and allow yourself to be affected by the various emotions that might come up (inquisitive, curious, defensive, euphoric, tentative, alarmed). Before you know it, you will both realize what great comedy energy feels like, as you drive each other to new heights of enthusiasm.

If you're doing this in front of people, *make sure you hold for the laugh.* This is vital in comedy acting. If you continue talking while the audience is laughing, you are telling them to stop laughing. As the laughter dies down, visualize an elevator indicator showing its descent. Just before it hits the next floor, you can start talking again.

This exercise forces you to stay in the moment. You cannot think about what you're going to say next. You must be present and LISTEN. Let the other actor's energy in and let it feed you and pump you. You are not a robot. You are awake and alive, with the natural instinct to be affected by another person.

The alliterations that follow are composed of four words that start with the same first letter. I've listed plenty of choices for you to play with. Your job is to be believable in every way. Take the four words you've been given, own them, and create a person with the kind of identity the words represent. Let your creative flow take over. Fully become the person in the occupation and allow different emotions to come up. Then mirror the emotions from the other actor as they come back to you.

Adept, Acidic, Acrimonious Acrobat
Better Built Brassier Buyer
Bippity Boppity Blues Bugler
Blunderous Bluesy Blithering Bluffer
Boston Bird Bath Builder
Canadian Chewy Chicklet Checker
Caustic Caucasian Callisthenic Calibrator
Chattanooga Cherry Chicklet Checker
Cheddar Chive Cheese Checker
Crab 'n Crawfish Cracker
Cuban Cuckoo Clock Collector
Dainty Diminy Dress Designer
Determined, Desirable, Diligent Dentist
Dixie Dugan Disco Dancer
Double Dutch Donut Dunker
Drip Dry Dress Designer
Ecstatic Easter Egg Examiner
English Exiled X-rated Exhibitionist
Filleted, Fluke and Flounder Fryer
Frightened Florida Fern Fancier
Frozen Fresh Fruit Fructarian
Gallant Greek Goose Grinder
Grumpy, Gratuitous, Grateful Grocer
Homegrown Hollywood Hotel Hooker
Hot House Hyacinth Hoser
Jelly Jam Juice Jarrer
Jubilant, Judicious, Jovial Juicer
Kumquat 'n Quince Crusher
Lemon-Lime Lollipop Licker
Lively Louisiana Lip Locker
Magnificent, Malaysian Map Maker
Malted Milk Marshmallow Mixer
Massachusetts Mental Math Marvel
Monochromatic Macrobiotic Militant Mechanic

Nutty Neapolitan Noodle Notcher
Outrageous, Overt, Organized Organist
Peach, Plum, Persimmon, and Prune Pitter
Pennsylvania Pickled Pepper Packer
Professional Poultry Produce Procurer
Proud Prickly Pear Packer
Quirky Quick Quip Quoter
Reprehensible, Repetitious, Resplendent Researcher
Ridiculous Rhodesian Rattlesnake Wrangler
Ripe Red Raspberry Rancher
Rotating Roto Rooter Rammer
Rude Russian Roulette Referee
Sassafras, Sarsaparilla, Soda Salesman
Schenectady Ski, Skate, and Scooter Scorer
Skinny, Saskatchewan, Society, Soroptimist
Sweet and Sour Sausage Stuffer
Taco 'n Tamale Taster
Tennessee Tic-Tac-Toe Tester
Tippity Tip Tap Toe Tapper
Venomous and Voluptuous Virginia Viking
Victorian Viennese Violin Varnisher
Wacky, Wirey, Wonderful Winner
Walla Walla Window Washer
Worrisome Wounded Wobbly Wrestler
Yappy Yearning Yeoman Yodeler

AN EXAMPLE:

Read the sample conversation aloud to get the feeling of the exercise.

A: Hello!
B: Hello!
A: Nice to meet you.
B: Nice to meet you.
A: What do you do?
B: What do I do?
A: What do you do?
B: What do I do?
A: What do you do?
B: What do I do?
A: I want to know what you do.
B: You want to know what I do.
A: I want to know what you do.
B: I'm a Sweet and Sour Sausage Stuffer.
A: Sweet and Sour Sausage Stuffer?
B: Yes, a Sweet and Sour Sausage Stuffer.
A: Sweet and Sour Sausage Stuffer?
B: Yes, a Sausage Stuffer.
A: You stuff sausages?
B: Yes, I stuff sausages.
A: You stuff sausages.
B: Yes, I stuff sausages.
A. You're a Sausage Stuffer!
B: That's right, I'm a Sausage Stuffer.
A: I would have never guessed.
B: Would have never guessed?
A: Would never have guessed.
B: Would never have guessed!
A: How do you stuff a sausage?
B: How do I stuff a sausage?
A: How do you stuff a sausage?
B: How do I stuff a sausage?
A: That's what I'm asking.
B: I stuff it.
A: You stuff it how?

B: *I stuff it with my foot.*

A: With your foot?

B: *With my foot!*

A: I've never heard of that before.

B: *You've never heard of that before?*

A: You stuff with your foot?

B: *I stuff with my foot.*

A: Most do it with their hand.

B: *Most do it with their hand?*

A: Why foot?

B: *It's better.*

A: It's better?

B: *It's better.*

A: I'm a Dixie Dugan Disco Dancer.

B: *Dixie Dugan Disco Dancer?*

A: Dixie Dugan Disco Dancer.

B: *Dixie Dugan Disco Dancer.*

A: I am a Disco Dancer for Dixie Dugan.

B: *Dixie Dugan?*

A: Dixie Dugan.

B: *Dixie Dugan.*

A: You know Dixie?

B: *Dixie? Yes, I know Dixie.*

A: You know Dixie Dugan?

B: *I know Dixie Dugan.*

A: I danced with her.

B: *You danced with her?*

A: She taught me how to dance.

B: *Taught you how to dance?*

A: Disco dance.

B: *Disco dance?*

A: Disco dance for Dixie.

B: *For Dixie?*

A: Would you like to dance for Dixie?

B: *Would I like to dance for Dixie?*

A: Would you want to dance with Dixie?

B: *Would I want to dance with Dixie?*

A: Come on, Dixie would teach you.

B: *Why don't we dance?*

A: I'll dance and you'll stuff.
B: You'll dance and I'll stuff?
A: We'll have a stuffing Disco dance.
B: A stuffing Disco dance!
A: Because you'll stuff with your feet.
B: My feet!
A: Your feet.
B: With my feet.
A: You could do a great dance with your feet.
B: With my feet.
A: And I'll dance for Dixie.
B: And you'll dance for Dixie.

PHYSICAL FREEZE TAG

This exercise enables you to use your body to stimulate your comedy energy. Much of comedy acting depends on physical humor. Actors need to get out of their head and work on freeing up, expressing themselves through body language. Nothing expands actors more than creating freedom through their physicality. To master this exercise you must be willing to tap into your "silly" and not worry about how you appear to others. To move humor along successfully from one player to the next, you have to be willing to stretch your imagination into physical positions that you may not have thought of before.

PEOPLE NEEDED: 3 or more

SCENE: Two actors onstage.

DIRECTIONS: Two actors begin go onstage, initiate a conversation, and get involved in some kind of physical position. An actor on the sideline then yells, "Freeze!" and replaces the person who has been onstage the longest by gently tapping the actor they're replacing on the back. The replacement should take the scene in an entirely new direction. Each replacement should happen quickly. Make it a brief interaction that stimulates your comedy imagination in some physical manner. As you improvise, you want to explore moving the scene into different types of physical interaction. Whichever actor on the sideline yells, "Freeze!" has to replace the actor performing the physical interaction at the moment, keeping up the same energy level as the person leaving the stage.

MATCHING THE EMOTION TO THE STATE OF MIND

This exercise not only helps you realize how many different ways you can enter a scene, but it also helps you learn how to pick up on the other person's emotions and feelings.

PEOPLE NEEDED: 3 (2 if necessary)

SCENE: Two strangers enter stage from either side with the same emotion.

DIRECTIONS: An offstage person designates what emotions the actors will use when interacting with each other onstage. Being present with each other in order to mirror the energy of your partner is the key to this exercise. If you don't have a third person, one of the two participants can choose the emotion. Below are some suggestions:

Angry
Arrogant
Bashful
Excited
Happy
Hateful
Hypochondriacal
Insecure
Loving
Nervous
Sad
Secretive
Shy
Tired

GROUP 2 EXERCISES: HONING YOUR LISTENING SKILLS

In the finest comedy performances, an energy dance arises among actors from the constant give and take that the dialogue, along with the appropriate feelings, demands. To achieve this relationship, however, the actors must learn to *acutely* listen to each other.

Many people go onstage with their mind racing with thoughts of how they want the scene to go. They focus on their own lines or on coming up with plot ideas to create the comedy that *they* want.

Unfortunately, when they start improvising, they find that within minutes the scene spirals downward. Beneath the surface, the actors are not reacting to the lines and feelings from their partners because they've simply stopped listening. For this reason, you must hone your listening skills to embrace what others are delivering to you. One good way to sharpen your listening skill is to practice it in your everyday life. Most of us listen with the intent to figure out what we are going to say next or how we are going to interject. Instead, listen with no agenda, as you already know what you know, so be open to someone else's view.

BIG NEWS

This exercise is a great warm-up to get your listening skills percolating.

PEOPLE NEEDED: 2 or more

SCENE: One person is onstage performing a physical activity at home when, all of a sudden, a friend excitedly bursts on the stage with big news about something that's just happened in his or her life.

DIRECTIONS: The person at home drops the activity and focuses on the friend's story, which has a little bit of absurdity to it. Below are some premises:

I think I just saw Elvis at the post office.
I may have won the lottery and can't find my ticket.
I missed my favorite TV show last night and I'm in a panic.
I fell in love in my dreams last night and I have to find that person—I know they're waiting for me.
I was visited by a UFO last night and they're coming to get me tonight. What should I take with me?
I think I've created the next great invention!
I think I have what it takes to be a star in Hollywood!
I want to become a supermodel.
I just did my family tree and I think I'm related to George Washington.
I went to a psychic and this is what they told me!

TELLING A STORY ONE WORD AT A TIME

This is a great but difficult exercise that builds your listening skills and helps you learn how to listen and react quickly.

PEOPLE NEEDED: 4

SCENE: Four people onstage make up a story one word at a time.

DIRECTIONS: You must completely trust each other and listen to each other with razor-sharp listening skills. This takes an enormous amount of effort. You're basically four minds thinking in unison, a team creating sentences and a story on the fly, one word at a time. Here are some generic themes to use so that the four of you have an umbrella to work under.

A historical event
The Bible
How to make a movie
How to find a relationship
How to be a detective
Politics today
The nutritional value of vegetables
How to cook great pasta
How to stay healthy
Disciplining your children

FIRST LINE/LAST LINE

This exercise helps actors learn to work together toward the same objective. An effective strategy to think about when you're acting is to take some of the focus off of yourself and be more interested in the other person.

PEOPLE NEEDED: 2 or more

SCENE: Two actors are onstage.

DIRECTIONS: An offstage person comes up with the first line for the two actors to start the scene. Another person offstage gives an actor the last line of the scene, which should have nothing to do with the opening line. One of the offstage people designates the location of the scene. If you only have two people, make up the opening and closing lines yourselves. After the first actor speaks the first line, the two actors must work together to steer the conversation to logically reach the ending line.

For example, let's say actor #1's first line is, "I love a great juicy pickle"; and actor #2's last line is, "I'm dating an ambulance driver"; and the location is a laundromat. The two actors might do something like this: Actor #1 eats a pickle and offers one to the second actor. The actors proceed in the scene naturally, but both Actor #1 and Actor #2 work together to veer the conversation to where it needs to wind up. In the middle of the scene they might look out and see what cars are passing outside the laundromat. Actor #2 plants a seed toward the end goal and states along the way that he or she is getting picked up at 6:00 o'clock. Actor #1 would then direct the scene toward the ending by saying, "My goodness, there's a loud siren outside." Actor #2 could then say his or her last line legitimately, "It's probably for me. I'm dating an ambulance driver." Some suggestions for locations:

Airport
Beach
Camp
College campus
Hotel lobby
Laundromat
Military base
Office building
Party
Swap meet

YES, AND...

In this exercise you learn how to interact with your partner and build a dialogue by completely agreeing with each other by saying, "Yes, and ..." This means that you understand and agree with whatever your partner says and then add your contribution to the conversation.

PEOPLE NEEDED: 2

SCENE: Two strangers meet on a park bench. One actor is seated onstage while the other enters.

DIRECTIONS: Either actor, or someone offstage, decides the topic to be discussed. The actors' goal is to agree with each other as much as possible and to continue to build the story together. Some suggested topics are:

My wife/husband is into Pilates.
I got a boss who is the biggest pain in the neck.
My director is an idiot.
I'm going to deport my mother-in-law!
I had the worst customer in the world today.
My psychologist is stranger than I am.
My father/mother scares all my boyfriends/girlfriends off.
My daughter/son is marrying an extraterrestrial alien.

I've been dating a girl/guy who's going to introduce me to culture.
My ex-husband/wife is going to run for mayor.
My neighbor is at it again.
TV is really an idiot box.
All of a sudden, my family is on a health kick.

GROUP 3 EXERCISES: RELEASING INHIBITIONS

Learning how to be completely free and uninhibited to say and do anything and everything is extremely important in comedy acting. Many people think they can easily do this once they get onstage, but I can tell you from experience most of us carry around a ton of inhibitions, which prevent us from living with complete freedom. As I related in the preface, it took me nearly a year before I could let go of the stressful anxiety I felt whenever I had to get onstage during my comedy classes.

Releasing your mind from all the inhibitions and cultural taboos you learned as a child actually takes a great deal of effort and practice. In the introduction I talked about peeling the onion to get to your comedy core and letting go of your inhibitions, which is one layer of the onion.

Becoming free to explore your comedy and create something new is vital in today's marketplace. Any actor who has auditioned for a professional part will tell you that producers will say, "Let me see what you can do with this. How would you play it?" An actor should be ready for anything that is thrown to him or her, as there are lots of last-minute changes to scripts, especially in TV sitcoms, which require the actor to act them with almost no time to study. Megan Mullally, the actress who played Karen on the TV sitcom *Will & Grace*, is a good example of someone who is free and able to create something new at any moment. Through her extensive background and training, she developed a unique comedic character that mesmerized the country. She knows how to use her voice and body language, which comes from years of experimentation and exploration. She is comedically free and ready to do whatever it takes to brilliantly deliver her performance.

The exercises in this group are the most fun and liberating exercises you can find as a budding comedy actor. Nearly all of them involve "improv bantering," by which I mean having two or more actors onstage that generate nonstop dialogue in a free-flowing, anything-goes manner. Learning how to banter to make the audience laugh is one of the best ways to release your inhibitions, because you have to be free to say or do anything. Bantering puts you in the *now* moment.

One of the keys to good improv is paying attention to what your partners onstage are doing and saying. If you're in an improv skit and are consciously thinking only about your *own* actions and dialogue, the skit will become stilted and dry. The best improv happens when all the actors work off each other, using each other's dialogue and action as cues. The goal is to keep matching the energy of the others so that you all stay in synch.

These exercises will also teach you how to use observation and sense memory, which means being able to visualize in your mind whatever you are talking about and to keep your senses alive. For example, if you tell another actor in your improv skit about a car accident you witnessed, you need to actually see it in your mind. You can train yourself to build your sense memory through practice. Look at objects in everyday life and then turn away and try to visualize what you just looked at.

Good observation and sense memory greatly benefits the professional actor, as there are many times when a situation or object may not be in front of the actor, and he or she will have to rely on visualization to perform the lines.

ANYTHING GOES FREEZE TAG

This is a great exercise to get loose. It prepares you to be, say, or do anything, as you have to be completely open to performing in many styles, dialects, and attitudes.

PEOPLE NEEDED: 3 or more

SCENE: Two strangers meeting for the first time at a party. One actor is outside getting some fresh air. A second actor comes outside and sees the first and begins a conversation.

DIRECTIONS: Shortly after the first two actors have begun their conversation, another actor offstage yells, "Freeze!" and calls out a dialect, TV style, emotion, or attitude. The two actors onstage must immediately switch into whatever is called out. Throughout this exercise, the two actors onstage help each other out by fully committing, to the best of their ability, to the switch that the offstage person yells. At the same time, they must also find the best possible way to seamlessly keep the thread of the conversation going while playing the new characters. This exercise will help you learn how to change on a dime. Below are some possible "Freeze!" changes to call out. Here are some suggested styles and personalities:

Shakespearean actors
Martial artists
Russian farmers
Incredibly itchy characters
Soap opera actors
Dallas cheerleaders
Passionate lovers
Rappers
Scandinavian skiers
Ballet dancers
New Yorkers with attitudes
Monkeys
Snakes
Lions
Hairdressers
Freezing cold individuals
Hysterically crying people
Hysterically laughing people
Models
Game show contestants
Sophisticated Britons
Indians
Southerners
Southern plantation owners
Little children
Older people
People fencing
Frogs
Angry people
Opera singers
Tap dancers
Adagio dancers
Aliens
Native Americans
Waspish Caucasians
Midwesterners

Suggested TV Styles:
Sitcom

News
Soap opera
Game show
Documentary
Miniseries
Police show
Telethon
Educational
Beauty pageant
Religious show
Talk show
Variety show
Commercial

Suggested Theater Styles:
Theater for the Deaf
Yiddish
Mime
Harold Pinter
David Mamet
Children's
Farce
Restoration Comedy
Performance Art
Broadway
Theater of the Absurd
Shakespearean
Kabuki
Cirque de Soleil

ARGUMENTS OVER A TABLE

This exercise develops your ability to be quick and spontaneous, and to release your inhibitions.

PEOPLE NEEDED: 4 or more

SCENE: A table is placed in the middle of the stage. Two actors are on one side of the stage and two are on the other side.

DIRECTIONS: An actor from each side gets up and stands on opposite sides of the table. One starts an argument with the other. One of the sideline actors then yells, "Freeze," gently taps his or her team member, and replaces him or her. The replacement actor must now take the scene in a completely new direction by either playing a character, using an accent, or simply playing him or herself. This pattern continues throughout the exercise. The sideline participants take turns yelling freeze, tagging their team members, replacing them, and redirecting the argument.

For example, if the two actors at the table are arguing about horsing around with the neighbor's spouse, the actor on the sideline might take the word "horse" and use it in the context of a racehorse and run to the table as a southern jockey, proclaiming, "I'm not riding that horse in the Kentucky Derby."

SHOW ME YOUR PASSION

This exercise gives you a chance to be passionate about something while completely abandoning your inhibitions.

PEOPLE NEEDED: 2

SCENE: Two strangers waiting for a bus.

DIRECTIONS: One actor, playing one of the listed characters in Column A, is sitting at a bus stop waiting for the bus. The second actor, a complete stranger, plays a character from Column B. The second actor initiates a conversation about their respective careers. If one actor is a prune dimpler, he or she needs to commit 100 percent to the world of prune dimpling. The actor needs to be passionate about the career and passionately share his or her expertise with the other actor. The conversation should move back and forth at a nice, energetic pace.

Column A	Column B
Prune dimpler	Tune stomper
Bird watcher	Grape jumper
Can stacker	Flag furler
Party pooper	Matchmaker (wedding)
Town crier	Wine sniffer (taster)
Porpoise communicator	Symphony conductor
Puzzle planner	Bird watcher
Lapdog trainer	Gas smeller
Union organizer	Cow milker
Cookie cutter	Party pooper

Symphony conductor	Nut cracker
TV tester	Potato chip picker
Grape jumper	Lap-dog trainer

AUDITIONING FOR A GAME SHOW

This exercise allows you to get crazy and wild. The bigger you can play it, the better.

PEOPLE NEEDED: 2

SCENE: Two friends at a house.

DIRECTIONS: Friend #1, after urgently phoning and asking for help in preparing to be a contestant on a TV game show, visits friend #2 at his or her home. The comedy comes out of the situation, as friend #2 works diligently to teach friend #1 how to play the game by role playing and acting out possible scenarios in order to get him or her ready. Be as physical as possible when acting out the game show. Both actors can take turns being friend #1 and friend #2. Below are some suggested game shows:

$25,000 Pyramid
Beauty Pageant
Celebrity Charades
Hollywood Squares
I've Got a Secret
Jeopardy
Let's Make a Deal
Match Game
Name That Tune
Queen for a Day
The Dating Game
The Gong Show
The Price Is Right
Wheel of Fortune
Who Wants to Be a Millionaire?

GROUP 4 EXERCISES: EXPANDING YOUR POSSIBILITIES

Comedy acting is the same as any other form of acting when it comes to the phrase "Your choice is your talent," meaning that when you go inside yourself to select something from your mental or emotional bank, you need to make a choice that moves you the most. Why select something that doesn't give you much of a trigger? Why not go for the gold?

As a successful comedy actor, you must have a large arsenal from which you can pull creativity. It's called your self-inventory. The way to build your arsenal is to master as many possibilities as you can. In this group of exercises we're going to help you learn how to:

1. Develop dialects and accents.

2. Be completely believable.

3. Play the straight man/woman.

4. Be able to talk about anything.

5. Show your charm.

6. Be authentic.

DIALECTS AND ACCENTS

One of the best ways to expand your possibilities is by learning to use dialects and accents. Being able to imitate the speech patterns and accents of people from many cultures and countries is the beginning of creating great comedy characters.

Learning dialects is more than just imitating speech patterns. It really helps if you can learn about the culture so that you can imitate the gestures and attitudes of the people. This helps create a sense of realism that the audience will pick up on.

One great story I heard on this point concerns Meryl Streep when she was preparing for the role of Sophie, a Polish woman, in the movie *Sophie's Choice*. Rather than using an accent coach to speak English with a Polish accent, she spent time with a woman from Poland. One day the famous Hollywood dialect coach Robert Easton was asked by his peers why Miss Streep hadn't used his services for the role. He contacted the Polish woman to offer his help. The Polish woman replied, "Vat do you know 'bout Poland? Vere you born in Poland?" Needless to say, every actor has his or her own way of working.

ACCENTS IN ACTION

In this exercise you're going to focus on helping your fellow actors. If one of you is good at a southern accent while someone else is good at a British accent, make an effort to teach each other how to speak it. One of the best ways to initiate strong comedy sketch characters, in the vein of *Saturday Night Live*, is working on various accents. And there's no better way to do this than this exercise, where you have to use lots of accents on the spot.

PEOPLE NEEDED: 3 or more

SCENE: Begin by having three people stand together along one side of the stage. Actor #1, who is farthest upstage (away from the audience), makes an entrance to center stage and immediately starts talking to him- or herself in an accent for about 20–30 seconds.

DIRECTIONS: Someone offstage yells, "Freeze!" and actor #2 (closest to upstage) enters with a new accent. To help the actor already onstage, the second actor might say a sentence or two to identify where he or she comes from as they enter. For example, the actor #2 may say, "My goodness, the shops in London open at 9:00. Why isn't this bloody shop open yet?" That lets the other actor know that the accent they are using is British. Immediately, the actor #1 adapts to actor #2's accent, and the two continue to talk for a short time.

Then, actor #3 makes an entrance with yet another new accent, and actors #1 and #2 must now adapt to #3's accent. This pattern continues if you have a fourth actor to work with.

Finally, move backward in sequence through all the accents again. This gives everyone the opportunity to try all of the accents in a continuous round-robin fashion.

It is very important that each actor makes sure that there is a balance and that all of them get a chance to talk with each accent, which is called *passing the ball.* It is also the responsibility of the actor who has a good handle on a particular accent or dialect to help fellow actors who may need assistance. One way to help actors master an accent is to have them repeat a short sentence, trying very hard to intently mimic back what the first actor said.

When trying to master a dialect, it is useful to exaggerate as much as you can, because it's always easier to tone it down than to do the reverse. After the exercise, have a discussion about it. When it's fresh on your mind, you are open to constructive critique. Help each other get a perspective on which accents worked for each actor.

If you practice each day on a specific dialect or accent that you are weak on, you will get better. Go to stores or places where an accent or dialect can be heard and see if you can get away with your imitation, perhaps an Italian bar, a French restaurant, or a Jewish deli. Tell someone who works there or is hanging out that you are working on the accent and see if they will help you. Compliment them on their accent and tell them you would be flattered if they would give you some pointers. Below are some choices for accents, dialects, and sketch premises for this exercise.

Some Accents and Dialects:
African
Australian
British
French
German
Irish
Italian
Jamaican
Japanese
Mexican
New York
Russian
Scandinavian
Scottish
Southern

Premises:
Visiting the U.N. in New York City
Waiting for an evening educational class to begin
Outside a department store sale, waiting for the doors to open
On a tour overlooking the Alps
Waiting for a concert to start
Waiting for the kids to come out of summer camp
Waiting for a personal-growth seminar to begin
Waiting for a supermarket to open
Attending a sporting event
Waiting to adopt a pet
At the airport
Waiting at the passport office

HELPING A NEIGHBOR

This exercise is great to help actors learn to be believable in a humorous situation. One person plays the straight man/woman, while the other person directly plays it for the humor. The first person is actually creating humor, as well, by continuing to seriously play his or her role. This can be challenging, as it's easy to fall into wanting to be funny and stop being believable.

PEOPLE NEEDED: 2

SCENE: A new house or apartment.

DIRECTIONS: The first actor begins onstage, playing the role of a homeowner or renter who has just moved into his or her new house or apartment. The second actor barges in, playing the role of one of the character choices listed below. The comedy plays out as the new homeowner continues to set up his or her home, unloading boxes and arranging the furniture. The homeowner tries to be as polite as possible while the pesky neighbor talks with an agenda and crosses the appropriate boundary of a sane neighbor. Some suggested characters to be played by the neighbor:

> A nosey neighbor who wants to find out the dirt on the new neighbor
> A flirtatious neighbor
> A neighbor who complains about the other neighbors
> A neighbor who just got out of prison
> A neighbor who wants to be psychologically analyzed by the new neighbor
> A neighbor who needs help with wardrobe choices
> A neighbor who complains about his or her love problems
> A student who wants help with his/her homework
> A neighbor who is a psychic
> A neighbor who wants to recruit the new neighbor into his or her religion
> A neighbor who is lonely and needs someone to talk to
> A neighbor who is into feng shui

HOW TO TEACH EXERCISE

This exercise will help you learn to become a master at talking about anything, at any time or at any place.

PEOPLE NEEDED: 2

SCENE: Two experts explaining a topic to the audience.

DIRECTIONS: Two actors enter from stage left and stand next to each other. An offstage person picks a topic that they must discuss. The actors onstage are "experts," and have to convince the audience that they are authorities on the topic about which they have no knowledge at all. They should work as if they are a stand up duo. Both parties have to be dedicated in their commitment to make it work. They should bounce back and forth, adding to what the other said. They can enter as characters from another country. So, if the first person starts talking in Italian, the other person must follow suit. The interesting part of this improv is to make the scene look seamless. Some suggested topics of expertise are:

Architecture
Chemistry
Electronics
Geography
History
Language
Law
Literature
Math
Medicine
Music
Philosophy
Physics
Political science
Psychology
Semantics (the study of words)

PROP EXERCISE

This exercise will help you to expand your repertoire on the spot, as it is an improv exercise that requires a great amount of imagination and spontaneity.

PEOPLE NEEDED: 2

DIRECTIONS: Gather a pile of varied props from among the junk lying around your house. The first actor stands offstage with his or her eyes closed, while the second actor places a prop in the first actor's hand. The first actor opens his or her eyes and takes five seconds to look at the object and come up with an idea. The first actor walks onstage and does a 60- to

90-second sales pitch. However, instead of saying what the prop really is, he or she must describe and sell it as something else. For example, if the prop is an old antenna, you might say that it is a device to communicate to aliens from other planets. Some suggested props:

> All-purpose cleaner
> Belt
> Bra
> Cell phone
> Clock
> Earmuffs
> Eggbeater
> Frying pan
> Hammer
> Magnifying glass
> Radio
> Scarf
> Spray bottle
> Storage bin
> Wrench

RECLAIMING YOUR CHARM

This exercise helps you discover your true, inner personal charm. One thing that's very important in acting is likeability. Tapping into one's authenticity is vital in your comedy acting. This charm exercise allows people to embrace the power of agreement, that is, to agree with the other person and to see the magic in the other person.

Sometimes, in comedy, people tend to leave out their unique personality and likeability. They sometimes forget how to be charming and can be rather robotic in their acting. Although comedy certainly uses exaggeration, it has to be based on a layer of truth. The actor has to be real and likeable. As simple as this exercise may seem, it can be challenging, because sometimes people lock their personalities away.

PEOPLE NEEDED: 2 or more

SCENE: Two actors onstage.

DIRECTIONS: One actor is onstage when the other actor enters. The goal of this scene is for the two actors to be as charming as they can. They have a conversation with each other and aren't concerned about being funny.

They focus on tapping into their own personal charm and talk with each other in great depth. They compliment each other, express kindness toward one another and notice everything about the other person in a most flattering way. Some potential premises are:

Two strangers meet in a cafeteria
Two strangers meet at a dance
Two strangers meet in a gym
Two strangers meet at a zoo
Two strangers meet at an airport
Two strangers meet at a campsite
Two strangers meet while on vacation
Two strangers meet at a museum
Two strangers meet at a bowling alley
Two strangers meet at an aquarium

THE SAME ATTITUDE

The purpose of this exercise is to help the two participating actors mirror each other so that both can benefit from being in sync with each other's traits.

SCENE: Two strangers meeting for the first time.

DIRECTIONS: Two actors enter the stage from different sides and portray two people who haven't met before. Each actor must feel and react with the same emotion or attitude. Some suggestions are:

Two extremely frustrated people
Two extremely angry people
Two happy people
Two insecure individuals
Two people who are very sad
Two people who love to boast and brag and are trying to top each other
Two very excited individuals
Two very nervous people
Two people who are very tired
Two bashful and shy individuals
Two secretive people
Two hateful people
Two loving people
Two hypochondriacs

CREATING A COMEDY NOTEBOOK

NOW THAT YOU'VE HAD THE CHANCE TO PERFORM SOME INTRO-
ductory comedy exercises, hopefully you're like my students and have
started to connect to your comedic core, discover your energy, and feel
liberated. My students comment on how they can feel their minds loosen
up, increasing their confidence about being funny in front of an audience,
after the exercises in Chapter 1.

The next step in exploring your comedic core is to create what I call
your Comedy Notebook. This notebook will serve as a repository for all your
ideas, thoughts, feelings, and visualizations that will fuel your comedy. It is
much more than a simple diary to write down ideas for jokes and improv
skits. It is more like a personal journal to give yourself creative free rein to
explore every facet of comedy that arises within you. Keeping a comedy
notebook serves five vital purposes toward deepening your comedy:

1. ENHANCING YOUR PROFESSIONALISM AND COMMITMENT

If you want to become a serious comedy actor, you need to heighten your
feeling of professionalism. As I tell my students, you need to fall in love
with both the *craft* of comedy and with *yourself* in the craft. This is
somewhat of a Zen concept to explain. I am talking about building an
attitude in which your whole life revolves around discovering your
comedic core and finding humor in the world around you. If you stop to
think about it, everything you do, see, and hear, as you go about your daily
life is material for your comedy.

If you're familiar with the great artist and inventor Leonardo da Vinci,
you've probably heard about the extensive journals he kept throughout his
life, in which he listed thousands of ideas he wanted to explore, sketches of
his inventions, and theories he had about the world. Leonardo, of course, was
one of the greatest geniuses of human history, and his notebooks are without
doubt a symbol of his fertile, creative mind. Keeping a comedy notebook will
transform you into a Leonardo da Vinci of sorts. In your notebook, you will
think, doodle, imagine, invent, search, play, visualize, and connect with your
comedic core. Your notebook is your private lifelong journal, where you write
down anything and everything that you hope to explore.

Many comedy legends kept journals, which I'll discuss later in this
chapter.

2. MOVING INTO THE COMEDY ZONE

For some people, being funny comes easily, at least some of the time. But
for most people, even those who are naturally funny, it takes a lot of effort

to develop a strong sense of humor. You can't just sit around watching TV or eating waffles and expect to consistently come up with ideas for comedy. You have to work at creating humor, and to do so, you need to get yourself into what I often call the Comedy Zone.

The term Zone describes a state of mind that successful people go into when they are creating or performing at their best. Scientists and psychologists have learned that during this state of mind specific brain wave and breathing patterns indicate that a subject is thinking and performing at a high level. When you move into the Zone, your actions and thoughts seem to flow naturally and effortlessly. When athletes go into the Zone, they achieve amazing physical feats; when musicians go into the Zone, they give virtuoso performances; and when writers and artists are in the Zone, their words and brushstrokes effortlessly fall onto paper and canvas. Whatever a person's talent may be, it shines through brilliantly with little effort. You stop worrying about forcing your talent; it simply comes through you.

Getting into the Zone is equally important for comedy actors—and frankly, working on your comedy notebook is one of the best ways to enter the Comedy Zone. I don't know exactly how it happens, but it works for many of my students. Perhaps it's the tactile act of writing that liberates your mind, or maybe it's the discipline of opening your notebook that focuses and motivates you to find your creativity. Whatever it may be, you will find yourself moving into the Comedy Zone when writing your thoughts down, and it will lead to positive results in your comedy acting for years to come.

3. INSURANCE AGAINST FORGETFULNESS

The third purpose for your comedy notebook is a very practical one: to ensure you don't lose good ideas. Most people find it useful to write down their brainstorms, given that today's world bombards us with TMI (too much information) nearly every second. Among the messages and perceptions our mind filters from advertising, billboards, radio, TV, computers, road signs, teachers, parents, friends, and strangers, most of us can't remember what we ate for dinner last night.

How many times have you had a great idea for a comedy routine or sketch while eating in a restaurant or talking with a friend, but by the time you get home, you couldn't recall anything? Many of my students believe they could have been the next Steve Martin if they had only written their ideas down when they thought of them. Well, the good news is that from now on you are going to have your comedy notebook with you, so you will never lose a single brilliant idea again.

4. CAPTURING YOUR FEELINGS AND BEHAVIORS

The fourth purpose of your comedy notebook is to have a place to explore and write down in-depth descriptions of your feelings and associated behaviors, which you can review at any time. Why do you want to do this? Knowing your feelings and which behaviors go with them is vital to all good acting, whether comedy or dramatic. Actors must be able to ground their character in authentic feelings and movements in order to be believable to the audience. You have to be able to correlate how your character might feel with real feelings that you have experienced in your own life. You have to be able to link the movements of your character with real movements that you would make in your own life when you feel a certain way.

This is especially true when you are working on something scripted, in which you play a role that a writer has created and recite dialogue that is not your own. If you cannot become the character you play, the audience will not find you believable. Even though humor comes out of the situation the writers have composed, actors must be able to make the audience accept the situation as being real. Thus, every action you do and every word you say must seem as if they are coming out of your own head; otherwise, you will appear to be a caricature of the person you are playing.

Your comedy notebook is where you will record notes about the gestures you make and actions you take for all the feelings you have each day. Your goal will be to explore your sense memory and to try and record the authentic movements and thoughts you had as you experienced the feelings. I will provide specific guidance about how to do this later in the chapter using a special self-inventory process I created.

5. CONNECTING WITH THE REAL WORLD

Finally, there is a fifth purpose in keeping a comedy notebook, which I call getting in tune with the real world. *Real* is the operative word here. The reason for this is that some actors tend to act, again, whether it's comedy or drama, in an unconnected way, meaning that they tend to talk from their head, not from real observations they've made out in the world. Their character often has a sense of being an automaton, lacking depth and authenticity. It's like they have never gone into the real world to experience other people, other situations, or other lifestyles.

Your comedy notebook forces you to get out of your head and go into the world to truly observe other people—checking out how they walk, talk, think, and act. These observations will help you build your skills in creating comedy sketch characters, speaking in dialects, and imitating the foibles and quirks of humanity that make audiences laugh.

Your Comedy Notebook

Here are the details about preparing your comedy notebook.

NOTEPAD

You will need a small pocket notepad to carry around with you. You can use any type of small notebook you want, such as a 3 x 5 spiral bound or even a little black book you can keep in your shirt pocket. You will bring it wherever you go *from now on*. Do you hear me? This is a habit you won't regret. As I just said, you will find yourself noticing more, thinking more, and coming up with more and more ideas as you begin exploring your comedic core and working with your comedy notebook. This means that you need to write your observations and thoughts down and then transfer them into your comedy notebook when you return home.

You may even want to consider buying a tape or digital recorder that lets you dictate your private thoughts and observations any time you want. If you do this, it is useful to buy a digital one that indexes your recordings. This makes it easier to find any single dictation quickly, rather than having to listen to an entire recording to find the one you want.

Don't feel self-conscious about walking around in public and pulling out your notebook or recorder to write or dictate your thoughts. Yes, you may be embarrassed that people around you might think you are acting to impress them, as if you were a major corporate mogul or a spy for the CIA, but there are worse things they could think of you. Recording your observations and thoughts on a consistent basis is part of the professionalism and commitment I spoke about earlier.

Steve Allen, a comedy genius, kept prolific notebooks. When I interviewed him on my TV show, he told me that he kept many small dictation tape recorders everywhere. He had one in his car, in his pocket, one in his office, one in the kitchen, and even one in his bathroom. All day long, he would record his ideas and then have them transcribed. It worked for Steve Allen, and it could work for you, too.

BINDER

You will need a simple three-ring binder, which you can find at any office supply store in your area, to serve as your main notebook. You don't need to get fancy. Three-ring binders are made in many spine widths, which indicate the size of the round clips inside. I suggest you begin with at least a three- or four-inch binder, as you will be using your notebook for a long time, possibly for years, and you want to be able to hold as much as possible in one notebook. I don't recommend using a spiral bound or perfect bound notebook, such as those colorful college-lined notebooks. A three-ring binder is more versatile, because you can constantly add new pages—and believe me, you will be adding tons of pages over time. Choose a notebook that also has pockets inside the front and back covers so that you can store loose sheets of paper, such as copies of comedic scenes.

PAPER

Buy any type of three-ring binder paper you want with three holes. Plain white, college-ruled paper is fine, though some people like grid or colored paper. It's up to you and you will discover what type of paper stimulates your thinking. Grid paper comes in handy sometimes when you are sketching, because you can draw a diagram on it more easily.

DIVIDERS

You will need a set of divider tab sheets, those yellow sheets of paper with clear or slightly colored plastic tabs attached. You are going to create five sections in your notebook. There will be other dividers you will create in the future, but for now you will need to create the five sections below:

SELF-INVENTORY
OBSERVATIONS
MIXED BAG
SKETCH CHARACTERS
ACTION SHEETS

THE SELF-INVENTORY SECTION

The self-inventory section of your notebook is where you are going to record your feelings and behaviors. As I said, solid acting comes from being able to portray authentic feelings and behaviors, and the best way to do this is to take an inventory of your own life.

Let me clarify this point. In the acting world, there are two schools of thought about where to find motivation when playing a role. One school believes you need to go outside yourself and use your imagination. The second school believes you need to look inside yourself and use your own feelings and experiences.

Personally, I believe the most powerful inspiration derives from your own life experiences. It's important to observe other people and imitate how they behave and move, but the most authentic acting you can achieve is, in my view, based on what is inside you. Being able to bring your feelings and behaviors to a role is what differentiates you from being "just" an improv actor versus a professional comedy actor. If you plan on a career in television or film and you aim to audition for parts in scripted sitcoms or movies, you must be able to work with someone else's words while also portraying them as your own. I think the best method for doing this comes from being able to go within yourself to know what makes you similar to your character.

So how can you get to know yourself? You can achieve this by working hard to take stock of your own feelings and behaviors so that you can ground your work and become aware of how you feel and behave in whatever situation you may encounter. Then you can extend those feelings and behaviors to the role you are playing.

I often explain this concept to my students by saying, "You can't mine for the comedy gold until you find out what's in the mine," meaning it's your job to go within and discover all the gems and jewels inside you so that you can become a comedy millionaire.

In the self-inventory section of your comedy notebook your goal is to recall as many events in your life as you can in order to recapture all the feelings and emotions inside you and associate them with the specific actions you did when you experienced them. To help you organize your feelings, you are going to create what I call Self-Inventory Worksheets.

Making Self-Inventory Worksheets:

1. Look at the list of feelings below:

Aggressive	Hurt
Anxious	Hysterical
Ambivalent	Innocent
Bashful	Interested
Bewildered	Jealous
Bored	Joyous
Cautious	Lonely
Cold	Lovestruck
Confident	Mischievous
Confused	Miserable
Crazy	Negative

Curious	Optimistic
Determined	Outgoing
Disappointed	Pained
Disapproving	Paranoid
Disgusted	Peaceful
Excited	Proud
Ecstatic	Puzzled
Enraged	Relieved
Envious	Sad
Exhausted	Shocked
Fed up	Shy
Frightened	Sorry
Frustrated	Stubborn
Guilty	Thoughtful
Happy	Undecided
Hot	Withdrawn

2. Write each feeling at the top of a page in your comedy notebook.

3. For each feeling, answer the question: When have I been [name of feeling]? When answering, think of an incident in your life, whether recent or past, and write what you did during the event. What actions did you take? What did you do? Be as precise as possible. Write down as many details as you can remember, and the feeling will become stronger.

     Here's an example from my life. My family moved to England when I was fifteen years old. I was sent to a "proper" English grammar school (equivalent to an American high school), where I felt very shy. I had to wear a blazer and tie to school every day. My classmates seemed to be about two years ahead of me academically. I truly felt like a duck out of water. I became shy and withdrawn, and I actually had to drop out of school after just a few months. I worked in a department store during the day and as a bartender at night. (The legal drinking age in England is sixteen, so a sixteen-year old bartender is not uncommon.) I eventually convinced my parents to let me return to Philadelphia, where I completed my high school education while living with a relative.

     What's important in my recollection is that I can still feel that sense of shyness to this day. I can see it vividly in my mind, and I can describe the movements and body behavior I assumed whenever I felt shy around my English classmates. I can still manifest the feeling completely in my body, which I can then use to portray a shy character.

4. Don't try to sit down and fill out the fifty-five self-inventory worksheets all at once. Take your time and do one or two of them per day.

5. Review your worksheets periodically so that you can continually reconnect yourself to your feelings and emotions. I assure you, this is the kind of work that can significantly expand your comedy imagination. The more feelings and incidents you recall and write about, the more you will connect with aspects of your personality that often lie unconscious for decades. You will come alive, and your deeper connection to your feelings will fuel both improvisational and comedy scene work.

THE OBSERVATIONS SECTION

While I believe that the most powerful motivation for acting comes from inside, there is no doubt that observing the outside world is a very important aspect of nurturing your comedy. You need to use your senses and observations to bring nuances and creativity to your work.

Many people seem completely oblivious to the world around them. For example, I go to a gym in Hollywood to work out and am amazed by how many up-and-coming actors are on the Stair Masters listening to their iPods. Very few talk or have friendly conversations with strangers, and as soon as they leave the gym, they immediately get on their cell phones. I find this limiting, as these young actors are missing golden opportunities to learn from people around them and to develop their observational skills.

The golden rule to remember is: You can't be a well-rounded actor if you don't participate in life. Spending all day escaping from the world does not feed your creative work. You must begin observing and connecting with other people in order to bring behaviors into your work. You need to move out of your comfort zone and begin to see how other people live.

Using your portable notebook or recording device, your goal is to note as many daily observations of different people and things you see as possible. Use your notebook as a journal to recall anything that might have potential to become a factor in your comedy. Whenever you go out in public, really look at the people around you. Notice if anything strikes you as funny or interesting about the way they walk, talk, or move, etc. Write as many details as you can in your notebook, such as where you were, who it was, and what was funny. These details will help you recall the incident with greater clarity when you review your notes later.

When you're observing, I suggest that you immediately imitate whatever it is that intrigues you about a person. If you see someone walking funny, go somewhere private and act out what you just saw so that you can transfer the movement into your own muscles. Physically moving your own body grounds the movement in your memory, and this sense memory will help you recall the event when you return home.

As I mentioned, don't embarrass anyone by writing down notes in way that makes them think you are spying on them. Again, there is that fine line between being observant and being nosey. Walk that fine line discreetly.

When you return home, transfer your notes from your portable notebook or recording device to your main comedy notebook in the observations section. Expand your entries as much as you can so that you can review them at a later date with clarity.

For example, here's a scene I witnessed a few years ago that I wrote in my notebook because I was working on a sketch comedy character. I love this scene, and rereading my notes always brings a smile to my face.

> I'm reading poolside on a vacation in Acapulco, Mexico, and a woman comes out from the lobby clearly making a "grand" entrance. Her very black hair is teased up almost to the 2nd floor of the hotel with a wing on the side that could have easily have had its own zip code. She was wearing backless heels and a black swimsuit cover-up, with bracelets up and down her arm that jangled loud enough that I am sure she woke up anyone having a siesta. Just in case anyone at the pool didn't hear her entrance, she yelled, "Harry, I'm hungry. Get me a hamburger." Her voice was a cross between Fran Drescher and Mike Meyers's "Coffee Talk" character.

I had struck comedy gold, and I was bringing it home!

THE MIXED BAG SECTION

In this section, you are going to record any and all those raw anecdotes, stories, ideas, and notes that you don't know where else to put—but you know you don't want lose them. You don't need a reason for putting anything in this section; it's simply material you want to save.

You can also fill this section of your comedy notebook with clippings you cut out of newspapers and magazines, such as funny headlines or articles that inspired you when you read them. There's no point in losing good material that someday might help you create a comedy sketch character or scene.

THE SKETCH CHARACTERS SECTION

This section of your notebook is devoted to storing all the ideas you think eventually might help you develop sketch comedy characters. We're going to discuss how to develop them in Chapter 4, but for now, set aside a section of your notebook for storing inspirations that can lead to your comedy characters.

One of the best ways to create a sketch comedy character is to cut out pictures from magazines that contain wardrobe and hair ideas that might appeal to you when you begin inventing your characters. Paste them onto sheets of paper in this section of your comedy notebook.

For example, let's say you are seeking to create a look for a character like the famous Austin Powers character created by the talented Mike Meyers. Mike found magazines with lots of photos of the 1960s Carnaby Street, London, look.

When creating sketch comedy characters, it often happens that the "outer" stimulates the "inner." In other words, seeing something outside of yourself gets you to brainstorm about a character that you can then internalize and bring to life from your own feelings.

The Character Bio Page

For each character you create in the sketch characters section, I suggest you make what I call a Character Bio Page in your notebook. On this page, answer as many questions as you can about who this character is from the inside out. Where were they born? Where do they live? What is their physical look?

I'm going to give you specific questions to answer for each character bio page when we discuss creating sketch characters in Chapter 4, but for now just place any material you find in the sketch characters section.

THE ACTION SHEETS SECTION

This section is where you will study and record specific information about the actions you perform in your daily life. Let me explain why you want to do this.

When I say action, I am referring to a verb that depicts a movement. An action is what helps actors learn how much variety they can bring to their work. The idea is to consciously study action verbs and think about which movements go with them. You can then rehearse these movements so that you can bring them into your body.

For example, if the action verb is "to embrace," you want to act out what it is like to embrace someone. When you do this, it is useful to over-exaggerate the physical action of embracing, to the point of overkill. You can scale it down later when you go to perform it, but the exaggeration helps your body remember the memory and the movement of an embrace.

The Action Verb Program

You will find on pages 45–46 a list of actions verbs that you are going to write in your action sheets section, one per sheet of paper. I have organized these actions verbs into a specific four-week program that you will go through. Each day you will perform the actions. Next to each verb you will find a few synonyms to clarify what the verb means. You'll find that when you enter a scene, you'll bring something to the table, which will make you more interesting to watch. This work is great for alleviating stress, as it psychologically heals the body and brings out your feelings.

DIRECTIONS:

1. Each day, take one of the action verbs and infuse it into your everyday activities. Fully express the action in your living room first. Get it into your body. For example, if the action verb is "pulling out information from your friend," make exaggerated pulling motions with your arms. After a couple of minutes, lessen the pulling motions to a minimum. The pulling motions will become anchored inside you, and you'll be able to humanize the sensation. You will be amazed at how much you feel as though you're pulling information out of your friend, because the pulling actions have become a part of you.

2. Transfer the words to individual index cards and place the cards around your house. You'll be reminded to do the same verb all day long, at home, in stores, or with friends. Start on a Sunday and select a new verb each day throughout the week. These actions are laid out for you to practice seven a week for a few weeks, until you master all of the different actions. Then you can add more of your own.

3. Practice each word on a daily basis, like taking your vitamins. I suggest you do one a day. Pay attention to how you act in your everyday life with the list of verbs. You want to get these action verbs physically into your body. This aspect of acting is not meant to be in any way a mental process. You want to take each action verb and act it out. For instance, when you extract something, what is the physical movement that goes on in your body? When you "embrace" someone, you open your arms wide and bring the person into you.

WEEK 1

CONFRONT: accuse, avenge, condemn, offend
CHALLENGE: dare, defy, threaten, demand
FORCE: compel, subdue, bash, overwhelm
CONQUER: overpower, quash, suppress, break
PRESS: drive, push, ram
DEFEND: ward off, uphold, guard
PROTECT: preserve, shelter, screen, shade

WEEK 2

INSTRUCT: develop, sharpen, shape
DIRECT: guide, conduct, regulate, point
RULE: dominate, command, oversee
LECTURE: drill, preach
STRAIGHTEN OUT: rectify, lay down the law
CLEAN UP: correct, purify, rid
ABOLISH: eliminate, renounce, clear out

WEEK 3

STRENGTHEN: empower, reinforce, toughen
RAISE: elevate, increase, expand, top
ENHANCE: perfect, improve, intensify
EMBELLISH: beautify, adorn, doll up
EXAGGERATE: magnify, embroider, enlarge
BUILD: establish, construct, create, mold
ATTACK: strike, lash out, fight, battle

WEEK 4

AROUSE: awaken, stir, revive
STIMULATE: electrify, inspire, enthuse
ENCOURAGE: urge, warm, hustle
CONVINCE: persuade, assure, sell, insist
PRAISE: acclaim, approve, applaud, glorify
IMPRESS: emphasize, penetrate, plant, pierce
ENLIGHTEN: enrich, cultivate, spread

Protecting the Sanctity of Your Notebook

Always hold your notebook sacred and believe in its value. Your comedy notebook is your private journal, containing your innermost creative thoughts and ideas. Some of the thoughts may be brilliant; some may be completely inane and stupid, at least right now. It doesn't matter; this is your creative work, and you want to protect your ideas as you think and rethink upon them.

There is no need, or value, in sharing your notebook with anyone in your life—not your parents, spouse, partner, or friends. I assure you, by preserving your notebook for your own eyes, you will be more comfortable writing anything and everything in it without hesitation. As soon as you show it to even one person, you will be hesitant to write your authentic, truthful thoughts and feelings down, which would be counterproductive.

Many of my students bring their notebooks to my workshops and discuss some ideas they're comfortable in sharing. But in this situation, the sharing is like two professional writers sharing drafts of their screenplays or teleplays. The exchange of ideas benefits them, with neither criticism nor negativity, as they both respect and honor each other's ideas. If you decide to share your notebook in class, make sure you are sharing it with a trustworthy classmate.

In addition, don't let other people know that you keep a comedy notebook or let them ridicule you or make you think that it is a silly waste of time. You may encounter people who ask why you are writing things down or who think you are making fun of them. Simply assure them calmly that you are doing creative work which requires you to take notes and that you are neither mocking nor insulting them.

I do recommend, however, that you use discretion in public. Don't stare at someone for long periods of time and write in a way that makes it obvious you are observing the person's behaviors. You need to be considerate, courteous about your note taking, and aware that you do not intentionally embarrass other people.

LEVEL II: INTERMEDIATE COMEDY EXERCISES, SERIES A

IN CHAPTER 1 EXERCISES WE LEARNED ABOUT DEVELOPING energy, performing improv exercises, bantering, listening to your acting partners, being in the moment, losing inhibitions, and developing accents and dialects. These basic exercises are your foundation to the art of comedy, and you'll profit from repeating them as many times as you can. Feel free to go back to Chapter 1 and repeat any of the exercises you want with your workshop, because every time you do them, the comedy will be different.

In this chapter, I'm going to introduce the next level of exercises that will challenge you even further and help you build your comedy imagination. These level one intermediate improvisations are slightly harder and require more concentration, creativity, and teamwork. But they also generate other levels of humor, because the situations offer you more opportunities to use your creative juices and exploit life situations for the sake of comedy.

To highlight the skills you'll be learning in this chapter, I've organized the exercises into five categories:

1. Learning How to Build a Scene

2. Playing the Straight Man

3. Playing Conflict for Humor

4. The Art of BS

5. Honing Your Dialects

Each of these categories contains several exercises. Many of them build on the skills you learned in Chapter 1.

Have fun with these improvs and don't forget to follow the Guidelines for Workshop Participants (page 3). Always respect your fellow actors and provide each other with support and encouragement. Begin by performing the six warm-up exercises on pages 4–8.

The Ten Commandments of Comedy Improv

Before you jump into the intermediate level, read through the following commandments to learn about successful comedy improv scenes. These generic principles pertain to just about every type of comedy improv exercise. I've learned and codified these principles from more than twenty years of teaching and performing improv. Each commandment is based on avoiding a pitfall that nearly always causes scenes to fail.

1. Never deny. Never negate your acting partner when onstage. It's better to work with whatever he or she may have said than to say something like, "No, that didn't happen." If you deny a line of dialogue from another actor, you throw that person off and the scene will lose momentum. Remember, one truth always follows another.

2. Keep up your energy. Energy is a funny thing; we can't see it, but we can feel it. As soon as you let your energy down, everyone will know it. Also, always remember that you must be heard by the audience.

3. You're always coming and going from somewhere. As you create your improv, always believe that your character has always existed. He or she was somewhere before the improv and intends to go somewhere after the improv. Believing this can help you create a background and future for your character, which can then be infused into the scene.

4. Every scene has a beginning, middle, and end. Remember to construct your improv around the rule that there are three parts to a scene. Maintain your awareness as to which part of the scene you are in as you perform the improv; it will help you build the scene.

5. Listen carefully. We take all take listening for granted, and it takes a lot of concentration to improve our listening skills. In your own life, think about talking less and listening more. You already know what you know; others can teach you new things.

6. Always be believable and let the comedy come out of the situation. Comedy is serious business, and your job is to completely surrender to the premise you've been given. Understand where the funny might lie, and then trust. Your job is to be completely honest to the scene and play it fully. Don't go for a cheap joke at the risk of not being true to the circumstances.

7. Trust and support your fellow actors. As we know in sports, it's all about teamwork. It's exactly the same in comedy acting. We're all on the tightrope together, so be the safety net for each other. In acting, it's all about giving and taking. You give to your fellow actors, and hopefully they will respond to you in the same way. If they don't, then your job is to help them get back on track.

8. Be quick on your pick-up by being fully awake and aware. As you improve in your craft and become more experienced, you will become sharper. You can't afford to be on autopilot; you've got to be aware of everything you can follow up on.

9. Don't judge yourself or others while performing. When you're acting in a scene you need every ounce of focus on what you're doing. Do not be distracted by your own judgments, as it will take away from your commitment with what is happening onstage.

10. Never negate mimed objects. If someone mimes opening a door, there will *always* be a door there. You have to honor that there is a door in a specific spot for the remainder of the scene. The use of objects and awareness of your environment greatly enhances the reality of the work.

Building a Scene

Of all the basic rules of comedy improv, one of the most important is that every sketch scene must have a beginning, middle, and an end. Below are the definitions of what each of these mean in terms of comedy acting.

BEGINNING

The beginning of a scene is the exposition. The actors define for the audience the situation or context so that the audience knows where the action is occurring, who the characters are, and a glimpse of what the scene is about. This doesn't mean that the scene must stay on the same topic or that other characters cannot join the scene at a later time or that you cannot surprise the audience with a twist as you move through the scene; however, you must provide the audience with a seed of the scene and identify the players.

The most important element when crafting the beginning of a scene is that you create a situation that draws the audience in and gives them a reason to care about the characters. As you improvise, you want to find some spark in your situation or in your dialogue that intrigues the audience and makes them want more. Not all scene beginnings have to be funny from the start. As you'll see through some of the exercises in this chapter, some comedy scenes actually begin with an argument, so it doesn't matter if your improv is not immediately funny; what counts is that you hook the audience into wanting to hear and see more.

MIDDLE

The middle of the scene is where you ratchet up the action, conflict, humor, movement, and dialogue. It is where you add complications, possibly introduce new characters, turn the scene in a different direction, or develop your characters in unexpected ways.

Not surprisingly, the middle is often where improv scenes fall apart—and is where you quickly learn that improv can be challenging. You have to keep your brain active, listen to those onstage with you, and talk while also thinking fast on your feet about where you can take the scene. This is why it's critical that all actors on the stage develop the ability to recognize when a scene has transitioned from the beginning to the middle. You must all work together to keep the scene going. The ten commandments of comedy improv acting can be very helpful for the middle of your scenes, because they teach you how to avoid the traps that cause scenes to spiral downward.

Energy is especially important when working in the middle of the scene. Once you've hooked the audience with the opening, you must maintain your energy—in fact, you want to try to increase it so that the audience feels the scene is moving. If you notice that one of the actors in the scene is sagging in energy, try to keep yourself from falling into his or her rut. Keep up your own energy and do something to support the other actor to renew his or her energy.

END

The end of a scene is its resolution. Some questions that should be answered are: How do the characters resolve the scene? Do they agree on something? Do they disagree? Do they agree to disagree?

There are two important criteria for a great ending in improv. First, always aim to make your ending natural and believable. Don't perform an action or say dialogue that negates the scene or bursts the bubble of reality that you just created. Remain in character and figure out how you can bring all the characters onstage with you to a credible conclusion. Second, aim to make your ending funny and memorable. Just as you want to hook the audience in the beginning of your improv, you want to complete the improv with a hook that makes that audience feel great about what you've just performed.

GROUP 1 EXERCISES: THE LENGTH OF THE SECTIONS

Naturally, there is not a fixed length for the three sections of an improv scene, because each one is different. However, the average length is approximately three minutes. A good rule of thumb to keep in mind is that you want the middle of the scene to be about fifty to seventy percent of the total time you are onstage, with the beginning and ending taking up the remaining time. Scenes that take up too much time at the beginning, with very little development in the middle and with a fast ending, are most often confusing and disappointing to the audience. Similarly, a scene that starts out fast and has a gigantic middle and practically no ending is also a big disappointment.

The exercises in this group are designed to give you opportunities to work on developing beginnings, middles, and ends.

THE PICK UP

In this exercise you will be guided by an offstage person, who will help you set up the beginning of the scene. It will then be up to your fellow actors onstage to develop the middle and end.

PEOPLE NEEDED: 5

SCENE: Two female friends and two male friends at a bar or restaurant.

DIRECTIONS: Two women are onstage, sitting and establishing themselves at a bar, restaurant, or other type of "pick-up" establishment. Meanwhile, two men offstage are waiting to enter the same establishment. The women might be:

> Women who feel their biological clocks ticking and are desperate to
>   find husbands
> Hookers
> Southerners
> A fun-loving girl trying to teach a shy girl to loosen up
> A mother trying to get her daughter a date
> Lesbians experimenting with the other gender
> Foreigners looking to obtain green cards

The two women talk for a while. An offstage person commands them to freeze. They stop talking and face the audience.

The two men enter and sit on the opposite side of the stage and start talking for a while, revealing their stories, which may—or may not—correlate with the women's backgrounds. For example, the men could be two men on a business trip, or two plumbers, or a father trying to help his son get a first date, or any combination you want. The two men talk for a short while, and then the offstage person tells them to freeze. This interchange can happen two or three times back and forth.

This is the beginning of your scene. For the middle, either the two guys or the two women walk over to the other pair to start a conversation. Improvise how the pick-up occurs in any way you want to build the scene. However, be sure to avoid a chaotic scene in which all four of you talk at the same time. If the scene begins to break down, the offstage person might dictate who is talking to whom: Girl #1 to Boy #2, etc.

Finally, lead yourselves to the scene's natural conclusion by walking out of the restaurant or bar and continuing whichever paths the characters would have gone depending on how the scene developed.

WINNER OF THE YEAR

This is another exercise to let you build the middle and end of a scene. It also teaches you how to switch your attitude on a dime, going from one emotion to another very quickly.

PEOPLE NEEDED: 3

SCENE: Finalists in a competition.

DIRECTIONS: Two actors are seated onstage, while an offstage actor controls the opening to the scene. The two actors onstage role-play that they are finalists in an annual competition that takes place somewhere in the world. Follow these instructions:

1. The offstage person interviews the two people onstage about the contest, letting them know that they only have two minutes left before the winner is announced. The two actors show each other how gracious they are and exclaim how the other should win. Below are some suggested contests:

   Best Pie of the Year
   Best Yodeler of the Year
   Best Plumber of the Year
   Best Ballet Dancer of the Year
   Best Sneezer of the Year
   Best Stripper of the Year
   Best Chippendale Dancer of the Year
   Best Pickler of the Year
   Best Gardener of the Year

2. Now you must transition to the middle of the scene, which begins when the offstage person announces the winner. From this point forward, the improv is about the reactions of the two contestants. The contest loser, who had previously been extremely gracious, now turns on his or her fellow participant, completely changing personality and venting anger onto the winner. Make up anything you want, such as accusing the winner of cheating, sleeping with a judge, or any subterfuge that explains why he or she should not have won.

3. Finally, figure out a way to end the scene, leaving the audience laughing.

I LOVE YOU EXERCISE

This exercise teaches you to build a character as you develop the beginning, middle, and end of your scene in a subtle manner. The exercise is funniest when you incorporate and embrace some absurdity into your character.

PEOPLE NEEDED: 2

SCENE: Two people in an awkward situation.

DIRECTIONS: Two actors begin by improvising a scene from one of the suggestions below. The actors need to establish the scene for a couple of minutes. Suddenly, one blurts out, "I love you," to other. The comedy arises out of the unwarranted and inappropriate time of the declaration of love. The other actor must deal with the proclamation of love in any way he or she wants, either accepting it or fending it off—whatever works. The love struck actor must then insist on his or her love and both actors continue from there.

For example, one of you might play a woman who is in the middle of ordering cold cuts from the guy at the deli. As they chat away while he slices roast beef, the woman finds an awkward moment to blurt out, "I love you." The actor playing the deli man may try to deflect the statement, telling her sheepishly (or beefishly), "Oh, I love you too." She might then reply "No, I *really* love you." And then the two actors will play out the scene end how they want. Some suggested situations are:

Woman/man telling a physical trainer
Woman/man telling a bingo caller

Woman/man telling a bus driver
Woman/man telling a masseuse/masseur
Rabbi telling a congregant
Woman/man telling a dry cleaner
Woman/man telling a manicurist
Woman telling her gynecologist
Woman/man telling a congressman/congresswoman
Woman/man telling a Salsa teacher
Woman/man telling a hairdresser

COMMEDIA DELL'ARTE IMPROV

This final exercise in group one leaves the entire scene up to the participants. Because of its difficulty, the actors in this improv get five minutes to
discuss what they want to do with the scene before beginning. Make some
rough plans about what to do for your beginning, middle, and end, then
hit the stage and see if you can create one integral scene that hangs
together. This type of acting is similar to how the actors in the Renaissance
Italian Theater, called Commedia dell'Arte, used to work. The actors were
given a story line and had to improv each scene using stock characters.

People Needed: 2 to 4

Directions: Using two to four actors, select a location from one of the
suggestions below. Go offstage and take a few minutes to conceive your
premise and the *arc* (the movement) of your scene. Create any story
structure you want. Don't spend time thinking about your dialogue; just
plan your story structure in terms of a beginning, middle, and end. If you
come to the end of your five minutes without being able to plan the entire
scene, you'll just have to give it your best shot. Here are some suggestions
for possible locations:

Baseball stadium
Botox party
Cocktail party
Dentist office
Gym
Hair salon
Hospital
Hotel
Library

Military recruitment office
Office
Pet spa
Restaurant

GROUP 2 EXERCISES: PLAYING THE STRAIGHT MAN

This group of exercises will teach you how to play the *straight man*—the character in a scene who appears not to have a sense of humor and who doesn't get what's going on. Whatever the other comedy actor does, the straight man continues to take his or her role seriously, never recognizing the humor arising from the other actor's jokes and actions. By the way, "straight man" is a traditional term in show business and is applied to both men and women.

Believe it or not, playing the straight man is actually one of the most difficult roles in comedy, and is perhaps the one that deserves the highest honor. Due to their ability to drive the comedy, there are many famous comedians in comedy duos who served as straight men, such as George Burns, who played the straight man for Gracie Allen; Audrey Meadows, for Jackie Gleason; Dick Smothers, for his brother Tommy; Desi Arnaz, for Lucille Ball; Dan Rowan, for Dick Martin; and Dean Martin, for Jerry Lewis.

The straight man is a revered role and carries a lot of power in a comedy scene. The straight man indirectly controls the action of an improv by forcing the comic actor to keep finding another way to explain or do something. Of course, being a team, the comic actor and straight man must play off each other, with a spontaneous give and take to help keep the scene moving, but a good straight man will actually run the scene.

There are many challenges to learning how to play a straight man well. First, the character needs to be believable, despite the fact that he or she must also appear more stupid, serious, or clueless than anyone would realistically be in the same situation.

Second, as the comic partner makes the audience laugh, the straight man must keep a completely straight face, never cracking a smile no matter how much laughter may come. Even the teeniest smirk or attempt to disguise laughter with a gesture will break the straight man character, losing believability and tipping off the audience that he or she is in on the joke, just like them. If you are playing the straight man and do break character, you must try your best to come right back into character. Audiences will usually excuse a momentary lapse, but beware; an actor who breaks character several times in a scene is considered to have failed.

Finally, the third challenge of playing the straight man is that the actor must find ways to be legitimately committed to the scene. This helps the other actors in the scene to build their characters and create the humor.

The following two exercises in this group will give you the chance to learn how to play the straight man. Take turns playing the straight man role, so that everyone learns how to do it.

COUNSELOR ON BOARD A CRUISE

This exercise allows one actor to play the straight man and be the set-up person for the other two actors. The key in this exercise is to work together so that the scene appears reasonably normal and believable, yet absurd as well.

PEOPLE NEEDED: 3

SCENE: A couple talking to a cruise ship's counselor.

DIRECTIONS: Two actors are a couple on board a cruise ship for vacation. Unfortunately, they brought their relationship issues along with their baggage and are fighting. With this background information, the scene begins with the couple knocking on the door of the ship's counselor in order to have their squabble mediated. The third actor is the counselor, who is the straight man. He or she needs to continually feed the couple seemingly good questions and give them guidance, which unintentionally intensifies the couple's anger with each other. The straight man's role is to keep the scene moving and to allow the couple to figure out how to make their argument funnier. Some suggested situations:

One complains that the other is busy all day long.
One complains that the other is spending all of his or her money in the casino.
One complains that the other is bringing the free all-you-can-eat free food to the cabin and stockpiling it.
One complains that the other is too cheap to buy bingo cards that are $7 each or 3 for $10.
One won't let the other sign up for the ship's talent show.
One complains that the dance instructor dances more with the other.
One complains that the other won't let him or her audition for the ship's amateur strip contest.
One complains that the other wants to go to sleep by 9:00 P.M. every night and miss the evening parties.

One complains that the other is flirting with the cabin maid.

One complains that the other keeps taking Dramamine pills for
seasickness and never comes out of the room.

COMMERCIAL INTERRUPTUS

In this improv one actor plays the straight man, a casting director who
unwittingly interrupts the concentration of two serious actors who are trying
to audition for a TV commercial. As in all straight man scenes, the straight
man actor must find ways to force the other two actors to keep churning the
comedy while making it look seamless and natural at the same time.

PEOPLE NEEDED: 3

SCENE: A TV commercial audition.

DIRECTIONS: The actor playing the casting director is onstage. The two
actors enter either as themselves or play any character they want; they just
have to be completely believable. The casting director starts and stops the
scene repeatedly to offer suggestions to the actors. Both sides work
diligently to frustrate each other, which makes the scene hilarious. The
scene progresses as follows:

1. The two actors enter and introduce themselves to the casting director.

2. The casting director asks them a couple of questions about their
   acting background and TV commercial experience. The actors
   improvise their answers.

3. The casting director tells the actors about the commercial being shot
   and what the product is. He or she explains to them that this
   audition must be performed without a script, which means they must
   improvise the commercial themselves.

4. The actors begin improvising the commercial. The casting director
   constantly criticizes the scene, stopping and starting it over and over.
   Of course, the straight man criticisms are intended to mess up the
   actors as they earnestly try to do the scene.

5. The actors end up frustrating the casting director, who now is acting
   like a director, constantly messing up or making them exaggerate
   their actions. Some suggestions for possible commercials:

Avon
Body hair waxing
Cialis (sexual performance enhancer)
Dental
Dog food
Equal or Splenda
Funeral service
Guess jeans
Gym membership
Japanese take-out restaurant
Kellogg's Rice Krispies
Liposuction surgery
Maxwell House coffee
Miller Lite beer
Mouthwash
Oscar Meyer wieners
Personal injury lawyer
Prozac (mood elevator)
Toothpaste
Toyota car
Vitamins

GROUP 3 EXERCISES: PORTRAYING CONFLICT

Portraying conflict is a powerful tool to generate comedy. We frequently think about conflict in terms of drama, but in truth, a good conflict has great potential to make an audience laugh. People are tremendously funny when they get angry at one another. They say the silliest things, give the most ridiculous reasons to defend their position, and reveal their deepest human frailties.

Being able to portray conflict for humor is a valuable talent that all comedy actors must learn. You will develop a wide range of comedy skills when learning to play conflict, including the following:

Moving from emotion to emotion quickly
Crying in a way that makes people laugh
Finding ways to cause other people's anger
Learning how to be annoying
Depicting petty thoughts and irrational behavior in believable ways
Learning how to exaggerate and nitpick in ways that are funny

All of these human foibles, when portrayed correctly, make audiences look at themselves more honestly and accept that anger and annoyances are often quite funny.

The biggest challenge of portraying conflict for many actors is learning how to do it in ways that lead to comedy, and not drama. When you're onstage, it's easy to get caught up in the conflict and to take it to a level where the humor of the situation can easily be lost. You have to be believable, but without making the audiences feel intimidated or frightened by the emotions portrayed in the scene. You need to learn how to gauge between drama and comedy much in the same way you must learn comedic timing. If you go too far, the audience will begin looking for drama and miss the humor; if you pounce too early, the audience won't understand the conflict, and the humor will be lost.

One of the greatest TV shows that created humor out of conflict was *I Love Lucy*. Lucille Ball was a master at creating conflict with her husband Ricky, maximizing comedy out of each and every situation. Her famous "Whaaa" crying routine is world-renown. Her seemingly innocent housewife character, Lucy, managed to find a way in every episode to annoy and aggravate Ricky, which set up all of those wonderful endings where they made up with each other.

Jack Lemmon and Walter Matthau are other examples of great comedy actors who exploited conflict for humor. Their comedy films *The Odd Couple, Grumpy Old Men*, and *Grumpier Old Men* are classic examples of two characters that cannot figure out how to get along. They get on each other's nerves to the point of an outright war, but their conflict is perfectly acted out to make us laugh at their credible, yet absurd, behavior.

In this group of four improv exercises, you'll have a chance to explore many ways to use conflict for laughter and experiment with situations and methods of portraying characters in conflict.

PETTY ARGUMENTS

This exercise requires you to use the skills you developed through the scene-building work you did earlier in the chapter. Your goal is to build a scene completely based on taking a simple, petty issue between a couple and expanding it to fill the entire scene. Like the famous comedian Jerry Seinfeld, you are going to learn how to make something out of nothing.

PEOPLE NEEDED: 2

DIRECTIONS: Select one of the issues listed below concerning a problem between two people in a relationship. Remember, enter the stage with a sense of who you are, where you are coming from, and where you are going. (I'm referring, of course, to one of the ten commandments of comedy improv: You are always coming from somewhere and going somewhere.) While onstage, the two of you must build your scene by introducing the petty argument and making it turn into a complete out-and-out battle during the middle of the scene. End the scene in any way you want, and make sure you milk your petty argument for all its humor.

One complains that the other never takes him or her anywhere.

One complains that the other doesn't like his or her mother.

One has moved into the other's home and now complains that he or she doesn't feel wanted.

One complains that the other dresses like a hippie.

One complains that the other never talks about a movie after they finish.

One complains that they should eat at home at least one night of the week.

One complains that the other doesn't balance the checkbook correctly.

One complains that the other had "roaming eyes" at their bowling night.

One complains that the other says one thing but actually means another.

One asks the other what happened to the romance in their relationship.

One complains to the other that there's no spontaneity in their relationship.

One complains that the other is too fastidious.

PICKING A FIGHT

This exercise has great potential for humor because it is based on the unspoken agreement found within many relationships: if one partner decides to be miserable, he or she is going to make the other partner miserable, too. This scene should show the audience how one partner can slowly descend into the same foul mood as the instigating partner.

PEOPLE NEEDED: 2

DIRECTIONS: Decide which one of you has the emotional hang-up and which one will be onstage first, setting up the scene. The goal is to play out the saying "Misery loves company." For example, a wife could be the happy person and is at home preparing dinner, watching TV, reading, etc.

Through her actions, the audience can see that she is in a great mood. Then her husband enters the scene, coming home from work or an errand, and slowly picks a fight with his wife.

JUST RETURNED FROM...

This is another great situation for a pair of actors to learn how to portray conflict while working as a team. In this improv, one actor will be the protagonist, instigating the other, who must maintain the conflict and escalate it. The two must build the story together, playing off each other to make the conflict as big—and as funny—as possible.

PEOPLE NEEDED: 2

DIRECTIONS: Returning from the list of suggested events below, two people enter the stage together. Begin to improvise that something happened to irritate one of you. One person becomes the protagonist of the scene. (Remember the first commandment of comedy improv: Never deny. The second actor must not deny the protagonist's story.) The protagonist must drive the beginning of the scene. As the protagonist builds the scene, the second actor can react in any way he or she chooses, as long as it escalates the argument. There has to be movement in the scene; it shouldn't be stagnant.

To complicate your improv a little bit more, you both must act out some type of action while you are arguing. For example, if you are playing a husband and wife, you might choose to be getting ready for bed while arguing. This will affect how you mime your preparation, which helps you learn how to be comfortable interacting with another actor while performing physical actions. Allow your physical actions affect the argument and the argument affect your behaviors. Some suggested events you have just returned from:

A dinner party at one of your parent's
A PTA meeting
A class reunion
A group therapy session
A doctor's check-up
An acting class
A cocktail party
A foreign restaurant
A marriage counselor

A Tupperware party
A screening of the movie one of you just starred in
Shopping at the mall

AN UNHAPPY COUPLE

This exercise offers another variation in portraying conflict. In this improv, you begin the scene with two people who are content. Then, little by little, a disagreement forms and quickly escalates. Your goal is to show the transformation of two happy people to two miserable people.

PEOPLE NEEDED: 2

DIRECTIONS: Two people are onstage acting out a great relationship from one of the suggested relationships listed below, or one of your own. At first, you are getting along very well. However, about half way through the scene, use one of the specific statements below to create a conflict. Decide which actor will make the statement and be sure both of you are aware of the statement that is supposed to ignite the conflict. The goal is to make the audience feel as if they have just seen a bomb fuse being lit, and they say to themselves, "Uh-oh, something's going to happen here." Once you set the conflict in motion, the dialogue should slowly escalate, step by step, into a big argument at the end.

Some suggested relationships:
Husband and wife
Psychiatrist and patient
Decorator and homeowner
A writing team working together on a TV pilot
Prospective mothers-in-law
Two astronauts in the module prior to take-off
Two friends reminiscing about school

Some suggested statements:
Let's go out to dinner on Saturday for our anniversary.
Let's get away for the weekend.
Let's have people over for dinner.
Let's get married.
Where shall we go on our vacation?
What shall we name the baby?

GROUP 4 EXERCISES: THE ART OF BS

The art of BS is one of the most prized traits of all great comedy actors. At the top of ladder in our generation is, of course, Robin Williams, who can rattle away nonstop on any topic in this entire universe, and other universes as well.

Being able to bullshit is an important skill to develop for many reasons. First, the ability to talk about anything helps build the acting skill called "acting as if." Any time you play a character in a role, you are essentially acting as if you are truly that character, saying his or her words with complete credibility. Mastering the art of BS will teach you how to say anything and have everyone believe you. If you can BS, you can be anyone.

Second, being able to BS challenges you to take your own personal knowledge and abilities to their highest level. Ironically, the more you know, the better you will be at BS. In a sense, building your BS skills for comedy actually makes a better, more intelligent actor and a better person. Your mother may not believe this, but it's true.

Third, which will surely surprise you, BS makes you better-looking, stronger, and sexier. Two experiments conducted by psychologists and scientists at MIT and Stanford, in which 100 volunteers with highly developed BS skills were monitored, revealed that the ten best bullshitters in each study showed significant improvement in muscle development, hair growth, eye color, and appeal to the opposite sex. Because of these studies, both MIT and Stanford are now offering their undergraduates the opportunity to earn BS degrees to heighten their career potential.

I hope you know that I was just bullshitting you to demonstrate my *real* third point: Bullshitting is a great skill because it offers you the opportunity for many vistas in your comedy. With BS, you can do parody, satire, political commentary, news broadcasting—or you might even land a job with the CIA or become President of the United States.

What does it take to become a great bullshitter? First and foremost, you must be able to create the appearance that you know what you are talking about. To create this magic, you must learn how to talk naturally without any long hesitations, facial contortions, and weird gestures that will indicate you are thinking about what to say next. Think about experts on TV; they seem completely believable because as they talk, thoughts flow out of their brain without strain or effort. They don't twist their mouths or move their eyes upward, movements that indicate someone is thinking hard about what to say. You, too, must learn how to speak fluidly and naturally, even when you don't know what to say next. When you are bullshitting, you have to keep talking while minimizing eye movements and muscle strains in your face.

Another ingredient in successful BS is the ability to use vocabulary that appears to be authentic in the context of your topic. If you are pretending to be a rocket engineer, you should sprinkle your words such as propulsion, G-forces, linear acceleration, mass, gravitational pull, and so on. Most people don't know if such words are truly the correct vocabulary of a rocket engineer, but they will tend to believe you if you have enough of the seemingly correct vocabulary. Similarly, if you are playing a brain surgeon, you need to use words like neuronal pathways, dendrites, brain hemi-spheres, ganglion stems, etc. People will not believe you if you begin talking about performing a brain surgery and say things like "I opened the patient's head and used the long metal probe thing to check out the white stuff with all those curls." There's actually a grain of truth in my BS tale above about how BS makes you a smarter person, because being able to use authentic vocabulary, which may require you to read more, *will* make you a smarter person. If you don't know the appropriate words, make them up and, most important, *believe* they are the right words.

The following group of exercises will challenge you to start learning how to BS convincingly. It might be a good idea to quickly skim over the exercises first to see if you want to read any magazines or do some research beforehand. A bit of intentional study might help you feel more comfortable performing these beginning BS exercises. The more you practice these exercises, the better you will become at bullshitting about anything without preparation.

WORLD'S FOREMOST AUTHORITIES

This exercise is much more challenging. You must pick a topic about which you have no knowledge and make it completely believable. This exercise stretches your comedy imagination and gives you great practice in running off at the mouth. By the way, this is based on a famous, old burlesque comedy sketch in which two people are running from the police and duck into a banquet room in a hotel where an event is in progress and the guest speaker is about to be introduced. To save themselves from getting caught, the two criminals (comedy actors) must pretend to be the expert speakers.

PEOPLE NEEDED: 3

SCENE: Two experts explaining a topic to an audience.

DIRECTIONS: Two people enter the stage from the side. An offstage announcer introduces them, saying they are the world's foremost authority on a certain topic. Whichever topic the announcer chooses will be the very first time the two "experts" know what they are have to talk about.

The two experts must work as a team to discuss the topic assigned. Facing the audience, the actors must flip back and forth phrases and small speeches that attempt to instruct your audience about your field of expertise. The idea is to completely play off each other, which makes it much easier for both individuals.

For example, if you are the world's foremost authorities on the love life of the speckled ostrich, you need to make it up as you go along. Whatever the two of you say about this topic, you must keep adding to it as you build your story from nothing. Try to get impassioned about your expertise as your story progresses. Some suggested topics of expertise are:

How to Be a Great Detective
How to Write a Comedy Show
How to Prepare a French Dinner
How to Throw a Successful Party
How to Pack for a Trip around the World
How to Be a Stanislavski Actor
How to Audition in Show Biz
How to Be a Critic
Bird Calling for the Hunter
Mating Calls of the Elk and Moose
Fish *Do* Talk
Dog Barks and What They Mean
Understanding Monkey Chatter
Training Your Bird to Talk
African Chants
Opera and Its Translation
How to Converse in Sign Language
How to Tell if a Diesel Engine Has Eight or Sixteen Cylinders
Modern Rock Music and What It Says
The Jazz Interpretations of Thelonius Monk
Ocean Navigation Made Easy
The Spirit World of Aborigines
Homosexuality in Guam

Heart Transplants
How to Run a Retirement Home
How to Cheat the Government
How to Be Successful at Anything
How to Run for Office
The Bible
The Family Life of the Newt
Bird Watching
Taking a California Vacation
Dieting for Sexual Pleasure
The Writings of Sidney Farber
Greek Tragedy as a Form of Entertainment
The Expressionist Painting of Angelo Fondue
Classical vs. Neoclassical Poetry
The Existential Philosophies of the Mafia
The Hippocratic Oath
The Art of Questas Folidair
Phoenician Hieroglyphics and What They Mean
The Comedy Genius of Ali Ben Hakim
The Crew Personnel of the Nina, the Pinta, and the Santa Maria
The War of the Roses
The Quantum Theory of the Sine and Cosine
The Effects of Gunod and Mahler on Modern Jazz
The Love Life of the Phineus T. Bluster
Running a Mental Hospital
Ethnic Relationships in Columbia
Sexual Life in Tasmania
Nursery Rhymes
Oedipus Complex
Semantics
Karate
Why Today's Youth Has Gone Wrong
The Origin of Marijuana: Its Original Purpose
Renaissance Art
How to Stay Married Even Though You're Unhappy
How to Raise Children
Lesser-Known Religions
Starting a Commune
Preparing for Natural Childbirth

OUR FIRST...

This exercise is similar to the previous exercise in that it allows the actors an opportunity to dive into their comedy imagination for successful bullshitting, while feeding off each other to help move the scene along.

PEOPLE NEEDED: 2 or 3

SCENE: A couple talking to an audience.

DIRECTIONS: An offstage person introduces a couple. The announcer tells the audience that the couple is going to talk about the first time they did something together. The couple doesn't know the topic until the announcer says it. The two actors enter and stand center upstage and deliver a talk to the audience about the topic they were assigned. If you have an audience of people in your workshop, let them ask questions to the couple at the end of the talk to increase the potential for humor. Below are some suggestions for first-time events:

> Our first date
> Our first affair
> Our first argument
> Our first songwriting hit
> Our first acting job together
> Our first vacation together
> Our first screenplay script
> Our first day on the police force working together
> Our first children's book
> Our first club-date
> Our first operation together as doctor and nurse
> Our first robbery
> Our first interior decorating triumph
> Our first romantic encounter
> Our first divorce

PUBLICITY ON EXACTLY WHO YOU ARE

This exercise gives one actor a chance to take the lead in BS. This is challenging, as the bullshitter must think fast and furiously—absorbing what is given to him or her and turning it into sheer humor.

PEOPLE NEEDED: 2

SCENE: A public relations spin-fest

DIRECTIONS: One actor is onstage portraying a public relations person who can get publicity for anybody, no matter who. Another actor enters, introduces him or herself, and begins to reveal true facts from his or her own life. Or the actor could play a working character, such as a carpenter, plumber, exterminator, or carpet cleaner.

The BS factor enters as the publicist must now take whatever the actor has said and embellish it to make it sound newsworthy. The publicist has the liberty to use any facts that the actor previously gave—twisting and turning the facts, finding a spin or a hook—to get the other person excited about how fabulous his or her life and career will be after getting the publicity he or she "deserve." You want to make the publicist larger than life, pushy, unrealistic, or whatever you decide to play.

GROUP 5 EXERCISE: HONING DIALECTS

As you began learning in Chapter 2, the ability to speak in dialects and accents offers you many new outlets for comedy. Audiences love comedy actors who can create characters from other countries and replicate their accents when speaking English, as well as their mannerisms, looks, and gestures.

To hone your skills in dialects and accents, spend time in neighborhoods where they are spoken. Pay attention to how the people move, their posture, what gestures they use, how close they stand next to each other when they speak to someone, the rapidity of their speech and the facial movements they make when speaking.

All of these elements of communication differ greatly from culture to culture. For example, when it comes to standing distance, Europeans tend to place themselves at a similar proximity to each other as Americans do. However, Arabs and Persians tend to stand very close to the person to whom they are speaking, practically nose to nose. Italians tend to gesticulate wildly, while Asians tend to stand rigidly and seldom gesture. Look for visual cues such as these that can make your accent or dialect be more authentic and allow you to fully embody that particular culture and speech. In the following exercise, you will have a chance to practice your accents and dialects.

A.M. SHOWS AROUND THE WORLD

This exercise allows two actors to practice their dialects and accents while also expanding on their bullshitting techniques. The exercise has an add-on module that allows yet another actor to join in and be an "expert."

PEOPLE NEEDED: 3 or 4

SCENE: Two talk show hosts on a morning TV show.

DIRECTIONS: Decide which two actors will be the TV show hosts. The two hosts sit onstage, getting ready to start the show. It is ten seconds before the show begins. An offstage announcer starts the countdown, five to one, and introduces the two hosts and the name of the show. In this process, the announcer reveals to the two actors which dialect or accent they are supposed to use for the entire improv.

For example, the announcer might say, "Live from Baton Rouge, Louisiana. Welcome to A.M. Baton Rouge." The location the announcer chooses is the first time that the two onstage actors find out which dialect or accent they are supposed to play. (If you only have three actors, the expert, who enters later, can double up as the announcer.)

The show begins and the two hosts take over. They must introduce themselves to the audience and begin creating TV banter with each other. They can talk about all the usual chit-chat that morning show hosts talk about: what they did last night, current events, the latest gossip, and any other mindless chatter that's fun and amusing. The key is that both actors must take on the dialect or accents of the designated locale.

The actors must play out the scene with a beginning, middle, and end for five minutes. The hosts can beef up the improv with guests who have been invited onto the show. Or, the two hosts can bring on a surprise guest or "expert." For example, if the guest plays an author, he or she might bring their book and give it to the hosts. The guest can choose to be from the same locale or from anywhere else in the world, using a different accent. Some suggested locales are:

A.M. Amsterdam
A.M. Australia
A.M. Boston
A.M. China
A.M. England
A.M. Germany
A.M. Ghana, Africa
A.M. India
A.M. Harlem, New York
A.M. Ireland
A.M. Israel

A.M. Italy
A.M. Japan
A.M. Louisiana
A.M. Mexico
A.M. Minnesota
A.M. Navaho Reservation
A.M. New Jersey
A.M. New York
A.M. Puerto Rico
A.M. Russia
A.M. Scotland
A.M. Sweden
A.M. West Hollywood, California

BUILDING A SKETCH COMEDY CHARACTER

WHEN TEACHING ACTORS, ONE OF MY PRIMARY GOALS IS TO HELP them achieve what I call "The Best Comedy You"; in other words, actors who've been stretched and expanded every which way and who can stand on top of their comedy. I aim to train actors to learn how to create their bag of tricks, to perform a wide range of comedy, and, most important, to know how to show both the truth and the comical. Producers and casting directors are looking for precisely this type of actor—someone who can show us both the real and the funny. This combination is what produces a comedy star.

To grab some of that sizzle, energy, and pop, you need to learn how to build one or more sketch comedy characters. A sketch comedy character is an actor's representation of a living being, whose persona, dress, mannerisms, and language all work together to make audiences laugh. When you portray a sketch comedy character, you are not portraying any of *your* own personality or habits, but rather you invent someone who lives outside of you. This character is a complete person who lives and breathes, has a personality, and is completely real while being quirky enough to amuse audiences.

An actor with a consistent and successful sketch comedy character may be able to write his or her own ticket to TV stardom. For more than twenty-five years, *Saturday Night Live* has seen numerous talented comedy actors who have created hundreds of memorable sketch comedy characters. We'll never forget John Belushi's Samurai restaurant owner; Dana Carvey's Church Lady; Dan Akroyd and Jane Curtin's Cone Heads; or Gilda Radner's Roseanne Roseannadanna.

An exceptional sketch character can even become the vehicle to a movie contract. Take, for example, Mike Myers, who created several block-busters and an entire merchandising franchise with Austin Powers; and Eddie Murphy, who turned some of his characterizations into the movie *The Klumps*; and Martin Short, who turned his Jimminy Glick character into a TV talk show *and* a movie.

So how do you go about inventing a sketch comedy character? Where do you find the ideas for deciding who your person will be? How do you flesh out the character and determine if he or she (or it) is right for you? And how do you build your character to make audiences laugh?

Creating a comedy sketch character is one of the most challenging assignments for the comedy actor to tackle. Coming up with the right character is work that requires enormous creativity, perseverance, and patience. You need to experiment and go through a certain amount of trial and error. My educated guess is that for every one enduring sketch character created in a comedy workshop, there are a lot of characters that were born and quickly died.

But don't worry. To improve your chances of birthing one of the survivors, I have created a comprehensive process to guide you along the way. Through my experience of teaching hundreds and hundreds of students, I have developed a methodical ten-step process that will teach you how to build a memorable and funny sketch comedy character that is right for your talent. If you follow these ten steps closely and keep yourself flexible and open-minded, you will master the process of creating multiple sketch comedy characters—perhaps one of whom has a chance of making it in Chicago, New York, or Hollywood.

Step 1: Sprouting the Seed

The first step in creating a sketch character is to find and identify a persona to be the basis of your character. You may not want to sit down and consciously attempt to write down a handful of funny traits which you then combine into one character. Building a character doesn't happen at your kitchen table or at your desk. The inspiration for a great comedy sketch character usually needs to come from the real world. The best characters are based on real people, because audiences love to see themselves or someone they know in your character.

To find your seed of inspiration, there is nothing more vital for you to do than to go out and observe the world. Look at the people around you everywhere you go. A great source of inspiration is often right at your fingertips, such as the people in your immediate circle, including family members, a spouse, a former lover, some of your friends, or even your enemies. We all have people in our lives who leave an indelible impression in our minds. They may be good, forthright, hardworking people who impress us, or they may be devilish, irresponsible, and childish people who press our buttons. It doesn't matter; either personality can work as a starting point for your character.

Of course, you don't have to restrict your investigation to people you know. You can base your character on an acquaintance you've met only once or even on a stranger you casually observed on the street or in the supermarket. Whenever you go into a public place, look for people who exhibit idiosyncratic behaviors, unique habits, or unusual walks. Listen for dialects, accents, comical expressions, and funny ways in which people express themselves.

For example, I went to see the hit musical *The Producers* in New York. During intermission, I was mingling in the lobby when I spotted a woman who immediately struck me as potential for a delicious character for one of my students. She was a short redheaded lady whose hair was high enough to have its own zip code, with a large wing spreading to the left that seemed ready for take off. She was smoking fast and furiously. I felt I had to say hello to her, so I turned and graciously said, "Hi. What do you think of the show?" Even though I grew up in Philadelphia and am definitely an East Coast person at heart, my years spent in Los Angeles made me forget the great characters that live in New York. In a husky, low, gravelly voice, almost like Harvey Fierstein's, she replied, "Of course, dawling, I'm loving it. What did you expect, dawling? It's *Mel Brooks*."

People like her remain etched in your mind and illustrate exactly how anyone you meet might implant the seeds of a sketch character. In this case, the woman's stature, hair, smoking habit, voice quality, New York accent, and her overly generous use of *dawling*, encapsulated a half-dozen traits that could easily be explored and molded into a character. Slightly reminiscent of Mike Myer's Coffee Talk with Linda Richman character on *Saturday Night Live*, this woman could be developed into a great sketch comedy character in numerous ways.

Before we move on to step 2, let me mention a few guidelines to keep in mind as you go about exploring the world in search of great sketch characters. First, use all your observational powers when you are checking out possibilities. If you see someone with a characteristic that intrigues you, don't just stop after writing only one observation, such as his or her clothing. Rather, try to get a sense of the entire person, because he or she may embody a whole barnyard of traits that can inspire you, just as my theater lobby lady did for me. Of course, you can certainly build a character by combining various traits from many different people, but if there are a lot of character's traits in one person, you will have an easier time creating a realistic sketch character.

Second, be patient and go for the gold. Keep observing and find the strongest persona that attracts you. When you discover the right person for you, you'll know it. Creating your character takes time and energy, so it's better to feel good that you've found something worth developing.

Finally, whenever you meet someone who might become the inspiration for your character, be sure to use your comedy notebook that we talked about in Chapter 2 and write down what you observe. Describe what you see in as much detail as you can. More important, I highly recommend that you don't stop at just writing down notes. Use your body and try to mimic what you see immediately. Go around the corner so the person doesn't see you, and begin acting out any gestures, mannerisms, walk, dialect, etc. that you witnessed. It's vital to capture the person's actions and behaviors and move them into your own body. Imitation helps you recall the movements more accurately and with greater detail. You have to *do* it, not just write about it.

Step 2: Test Drive Your Potential Character

As you seek out seeds of inspiration and find one or more candidates who seem like possible models for your character, you want to go home and begin testing them out. Like shopping for cars, it's worthwhile to test drive a few so that you can decide which one you ultimately want to drive.

Test driving a potential sketch comedy character means that you put yourself in the driver's seat and step on it! You have to make your character come alive by putting yourself completely into the physical and emotional space of the character. In the privacy of your own home, with no one around, you need to begin practicing *being* the person or persons you observed. Don't worry about what is or isn't funny just yet. Simply explore the ways you can go about mimicking and impersonating your subject(s).

Using your body, capture the physical nature of the person: how he or she talks, walks, stands, gestures, and any other essential aspect. Your goal is to absorb the person into your blood. Close your eyes and picture the person you want to mimic. Lose yourself completely and let the subject completely overtake you. In other words, channel the person. If you're playing the opposite gender, don't hold back; let your inhibitions fall completely by the wayside.

Manifesting someone else's body is what will set you apart from yourself. And that's what you want to do. Free yourself from who you are and give your new person the chance to take over. We all have the ability to mimic. Talk exactly as your person would talk. Walk just like your person would. Try to imagine what your person talks about. If the person was just a passing acquaintance, make a guess about what he or she might say to you if you had a conversation at a cocktail party. This is where your comedy imagination comes into play. For instance, if you met my theater lady at a posh New York party at a gorgeous upper Manhattan penthouse, you could try to imagine her moving around the party, with her sky-high hair bumping into the glass chandelier each time she crosses from one side of the room to another and a trail of cigarette smoke following behind her.

Begin to turn the person into a potential character, extending the imaginary conversations for as long as you can until you feel completely comfortable being the character. Practice it a few times. Believe me, you'll know when you're done test driving, because your character will take over your body and mind and you'll love being him or her—maybe even more than yourself. You'll experience a creative "Ah ha" moment when you nail the character in this initial test.

Step 3: Flesh Out Your Character with a Full Bio

Your character is slowly coming alive, but is still not fully formed. You now need to make your character "real." As I've said many times, your comedy needs to be grounded in reality; otherwise, you will portray just a one-dimensional caricature that appears to be cardboard and dull to audiences. When you play your character, you want to *be* who he or she is and *feel* what he or she feels.

The best way to flesh out your character is to construct what I call a Character Bio Page. This allows you to invent a background for your character in order to anchor him or her in your mind. You want to go inside the character and spell out his or her life story, as well as all the strengths and weaknesses that make the character human. These details will help you deepen your portrayal of the character, because he or she will become real to you. Knowing your character is the mechanism by which you can truly think and be the character. And as a side benefit of writing a character bio, you also develop greater observational powers and a better understanding of people in general.

The Character Bio Page is a written summary of your character's essential traits. To prepare the bio page, begin asking yourself questions about your character. Below are some examples of questions you might want to ask, but feel free to supplement these with any other questions you want:

What is his/her age?
Is he/she married or single?
Where did he/she go to school?
Does he/she have kids?
What does he/she do for a living?
What does he/she eat and how often?
Is he/she an Internet dating maniac?

With whom does he/she have a relationship?

How does he/she wear her hair?

What type of makeup does she wear?

What is his/her clothing like?

Does he/she dress well or slovenly?

What type of shoes does he/she wear?

What colors make him/her look great? Which ones make him/her look funny?

Does he/she wear a hat?

What does he/she carry around with her?

How does he/she get along with men?

How does he/she get along with women?

Does he have a beard or mustache?

Is he/she overweight or underweight? Where does he/she carry his weight?

Is he/she hip or old-fashioned?

Does he/she have a sense of style or is he clueless with fashion?

Is he/she nervous or easy going?

Once you've thought about all these types of questions, you're ready to fill out the Character Bio Page on the next page. I suggest you photocopy it and create one for each character you develop. Then place it in your comedy notebook for permanent storage. You never know when you might want to revisit a character you created in the past and bring it back to life.

You'll notice that one of the fill-in blanks on the Character Bio Page asks you to give your character a two-word description. I ask you to do this because it is very useful if you can capture the essence of your character in just two punchy, terse words. Whenever you play the character, these two words will help you launch quickly into the persona. Take your time coming up with these two words, and don't be afraid to use a thesaurus until you find the perfect two.

THE CHARACTER BIO PAGE

NAME OF CHARACTER _____

AGE _____   WHERE WAS HE/SHE BORN? _____

WHERE WAS HE/SHE RAISED? _____

WHERE DOES HE/SHE LIVE? _____

WHAT IS HIS/HER OCCUPATION? _____

GIVE HIM/HER A TWO-WORD (ADJECTIVE & VERB) DESCRIPTION
(Examples: Angry Tribesman, Gay Lieutenant, Snotty Socialite)

_____

LIST HIS/HER IDIOSYNCRASIES _____

_____

WHAT DOES THE CHARACTER LOOK LIKE? _____

_____

_____

DESCRIBE HIS/HER WARDROBE _____

_____

HOW DOES THE CHARACTER WEAR HIS/HER HAIR AND MAKEUP?

_____

_____

_____

In addition to the Character Bio Page, another aspect of fleshing out your character is to select some physical and mental descriptors that you want to apply to the character. Characters, like humans, are multifaceted, exhibiting a range of emotions and feelings. And also like humans, characters come in a range of personalities. It helps if you can narrow down your character to a few descriptive adjectives so that you can focus on developing his or her personality and physical traits. On the next couple of pages you will find a list of common adjectives used to describe a person. Use them to give yourself a visual medium to define and develop your character. Try to narrow down your selection to one or two adjectives; however, if you feel your character needs a few more, by all means add them.

Absolute	Coquet	Essential
Absorbing	Courteous	Excellent
Acceptable	Cozy	Extravagant
Adaptable	Crafty	Extreme
Adequate	Crazy	Fabulous
Adorable	Crisp	Fair
Alert	Cultured	Fancy
Amorous	Curious	Fantastic
Amusing	Cute	Fascinating
Angelic	Dainty	Feasible
Appealing	Darling	Fine
Artful	Dear	Flexible
Aspiring	Decent	Flirtatious
Astute	Dedicated	Folksy
Average	Deep	Forgiving
Aware	Delicate	Fragile
Bashful	Dependable	Fresh
Beloved	Dependent	Friendly
Beneficial	Desirable	Frivolous
Bold	Determined	Funny
Brainy	Devilish	Gay
Breezy	Devoted	Gentle
Bright	Diligent	God-like
Brisk	Disciplined	Harmless
Captivating	Distinctive	Harmonious
Caring	Distinguished	Health Conscious
Charming	Divine	Heartfelt
Cheerful	Dreamy	Heavenly
Clean	Dynamic	Helpful
Clever	Eager	Homey
Clinical	Easy	Honest
Colorful	Ecstatic	Hopeful
Colossal	Efficient	Humble
Comfortable	Electric	Humdinger
Comical	Elegant	Humorous
Compassionate	Elementary	Hunky-dory
Concerned	Eloquent	Ideal
Confident	Eminent	Immense
Cool	Enormous	Important

Independent

Infallible

Infinite

Innocent

Intelligent

Intense

Juicy

Keen

Knock out

Lighthearted

Lively

Lovely

Loving

Magical

Magnetic

Magnificent

Mediocre

Mischievous

Modest

Momentous

Neat

Noble

Obvious

Okay

Open

Optimistic

Ordinary

Outgoing

Passable

Patient

Placid

Plain

Plausible

Pleasant

Pliable

Polite

Positive

Powerful

Present

Princely

Profitable

Prominent

Pure

Rapturous

Rare

Rascal

Real

Reasonable

Refreshing

Reserved

Restful

Rich

Romantic

Rosy

Sagacious

Self-Promoting

Sensitive

Serene

Severe

Sharp

Ship-shape

Shrewd

Shy

Significant

Silly

Simple

Sincere

Sleek

Slick

Slippery

Sly

Smart

Smooth

Snappy

Soft

Solid

Spacious

Spirited

Spiritual

Splendid

Spotless

Spry

Spunky

Stately

Stupendous

Stylish

Successful

Sumptuous

Sweet

Swell

Swinging

Tempting

Tenacious

Tender

Terrific

Thick

Thoughtful

Tidy

Typical

Understanding

Uninhibited

Unique

Uplifting

Virtuous

Warm

Whimsical

Winning

Wise

Wonderful

Step 4: Dress and Accessorize Your Character

Now that you've done your homework to build an understanding of your character, you're ready to bring him or her into a more palpable existence. This work is challenging, but a lot of fun, because you now begin applying a physical look to your character. In this step, you will pick out the wardrobe, hairstyle, and any accessories that your character might have.

Where do you get ideas for your character's physical appearance? One good starting point may be found in your comedy notebook. If you've stored magazine and newspaper clippings in your notebook, go back and review them and check if any photos or images you've collected appear relevant to your character. Perhaps you've already cut out a funny photo of an ugly checkered shirt or a horribly designed dress that is perfect for your character, or even a picture of a person with the weirdest hat you've ever seen. You'll be amazed at the synchronicity that often happens when you invent a comedy character and the notes in your comedy notebook coincide.

In terms of buying the clothes and accessories for your character, I highly recommend that you avoid spending a huge amount of money. Definitely don't go into expensive stores to buy your costume, as this type of shopping is usually counterproductive. If you dress your character as if he or she were walking around your town, your audience will think you've invented a character that can found anywhere and everywhere. It's better to dress your character in clothing that's a bit off, so that the audience will notice something is askew. From a financial point of view, you can save money, too, by dressing and accessorizing your character with inexpensive or used items.

In my experience, the best places to find and buy costumes and wigs are at yard sales, garage sales, second-hand stores, vintage stores, etc. If you live in a larger city, you can often find the best discount stores in the less expensive neighborhoods, where the locals tend to buy clothing from mom-and-pop, surplus, and discount stores. One other piece of advice: Don't shop at costume stores, where people go to buy Halloween costumes. You are not trying to dress your character as if he or she were going to a Halloween party.

If you are involved in a comedy workshop, one fun way for everyone to obtain clothing for their characters is to have a workshop clothing swap. Get everyone in your workshop to bring in their unwanted and old clothing from home. Trade items for free; don't put dollar values on any of it. Just bring it all in, spread it all out, and make it a free-for-all, letting everyone choose what he or she wants. You'll be amazed at how much good stuff people have, as well as the great ideas that another actor's old clothes may bring you. In my classes, I bring in wardrobe items, wigs, props, and tons of junk, and let my students grab what they want. Even if you don't find something you want, you may at least become inspired by something you see someone else wearing.

As you go through this process, aim to assemble a complete wardrobe for your character. Be experimental, trying on a pair of pants with different tops, then substituting the pants for another pair. It's like those books with triple-cut-pages you had when you were a kid, where you would flip between the top, middle, and bottom pages to make zillions of combinations between animals and people. Stand in front of a mirror and make yourself into one of these cut-up books, trying on different props until you find the right combination that screams, "Hey, this is my character!"

The advantage of seeing your character fully dressed is that you will now feel completely authentic. It is the birth of your character, and you will begin anew to explore the character's behavior. In fact, sometimes the costume will inspire you with new ideas for your character, and you'll have to make adjustments to improve it. It can also work the other way, too, in which your character requires you to go back to the drawing board and find a different costume than the one you first selected. Just keep yourself open to the gestalt of the process. As in life, sometimes what's outside drives the inside, and sometimes what's inside drives the outside.

Be sensitive to how you feel about your character and your costume, because your feelings will tell you when you've nailed it. You'll know when it feels right, because there is a magical feeling that overcomes you. Trust me, it's true. When you get it, you know it, and you'll find everyone around you also giving you the comedy character seal of approval.

Step 5: Introduce Your Character to the World

By now you are probably eager and ready to introduce your character to the public. Unless you've shared your character with a few friends in the privacy of your home, this will be the first time that you actually display your character to others. Believe me; this event is so exciting that you are going to feel like an expectant parent. But don't be nervous or let your anxiety take over. When you enter your workshop, get into your character and stay in it for as long as you can. Repeat to yourself the two- or three-word description of your character that you created in step 3 for your Character Bio Page to remind you of who you are.

Here is the process I created for actors to introduce their comedy characters to their workshop mates. The process is a simple Q & A interview format, where someone interviews your character. Below are three methods you can use to do the interview. Choose any of them, or perform all three; it's up to you to decide which method makes you feel the most comfortable. After the interview, be sure to ask your audience for any feedback. Don't act defensively about your character. It doesn't do any good to defend your position to the audience about why you chose this costume or why you had your character do such and such. It is far better to listen carefully and be open to their suggestions. While you don't have to take any of them, what your workshop mates or private audience will tell you now is probably indicative of what any public audience might say.

Most important, your audience may suggest ideas that you haven't even thought of. Everyone has reactions and thoughts. While some suggestions may be way out, and it may seem as though the person offering them is a complete idiot who didn't get your character at all, others may be extremely helpful. Remember, feedback is critical for all comedy actors. Cherish and honor the perceptions and comments others volunteer. Say thank you—no matter what they say. And, when it's your turn to provide feedback to other actors, don't harbor any ill will or try to get even with someone. Don't forget that your workshop is a creative community and you must respect and work with each other.

METHOD 1: MAN-ON-THE-STREET INTERVIEW

Ask one actor in your group to play the role of a man-on-the-street reporter. The actor positions him or herself in the center of the stage. You enter the stage in character and fully dressed. Keep in mind that you *are* the character; you are not playing the character.

Next, as you walk across the stage, the reporter stops you and asks you some questions, as if he or she were a roving TV reporter, looking for people to interview. The goal for the reporter is to play the straight man and to give you center stage. The reporter needs to ask you questions that allow you to reveal your character. This means asking open questions, not yes/no questions. The questions need to give you a chance to talk about who you are and what your life is.

An Important Note: As you perform this exercise, position yourself so that you are in the center of the stage, facing downstage toward the audience. The reporter should face slightly upstage toward you. This positioning will help you learn to "play out," meaning that you face the audience in a way that holds their focus. Meanwhile, the reporter takes on a supporting role by facing slightly upstage. Below are some sample questions the reporter might ask:

What's your name and where are you from?

What were you doing before coming here? (Remember, you, as a character, always existed in the past and will always exist in the future. You are coming from someplace and going somewhere. So answer this question imagining what your character was doing and will be doing next.)

Where are you going?

What kind of work do you do?

How do you do what you do? (This question allows you to talk at length and, even better, to act out your job. For instance, if you say you are a chef in an Italian restaurant, go through the motions of showing the audience what you do. Be a chef; gesture how you toss a pizza dough or mix a salad.)

METHOD 2: CRUISE DIRECTOR INTERVIEW

This method of interviewing is a variation of the man-on-the-street reporter from method one above, but offers a more colorful context in which to introduce your character.

Imagine you are embarking on a singles cruise, like on the TV show *Love Boat*. As you enter the boat (the stage), another actor from your workshop is onstage playing the role of the cruise director and checking you in. As in method one, the role of the cruise director is to ask you questions that elicit long responses from you to help you reveal your character. The cruise director allows you to take center stage and play out as he or she asks questions. Below are some possible questions:

What is your name and what do you do for a living?

What type of mate are you looking for on this cruise?

Where are you from?

What are your hobbies?

METHOD 3: REALITY SHOW INTERVIEW

A third way to conduct your character interview uses the reality TV show concept. You begin onstage by yourself. Meanwhile, another actor sits in the audience and plays a producer of a reality TV show. He or she tells you that the network is looking for interesting guests for a new show. As in methods one and two above, the reality show producer must interview you in a way that allows you to open up and answer questions to reveal your character.

The difference between this interview method and the two above is that you are alone onstage, since the interviewer sits in the audience. Working solo puts you completely in the spotlight, unlike the previous two methods. This method is far more challenging, since you have no physical presence to shield or support you while onstage. All eyes are on you, so every gesture and action you make takes on a greater importance.

The advantage of this interview method is that you own the stage and can do and say whatever you want. Below are some sample questions for the interviewer:

> Do you have any special talents for the reality show? What are they and can you show us them?
> Do you have any unusual or interesting habits?
> What are you hobbies?
> What was your life like growing up?
> Who are some of your friends? What are they like?

Step 6: Record Your Character Using Photos and Video

Either during or after the interview, begin to record or snap some photos of your character in various environments and at different angles. When interviewing, you may want to ask if someone could bring a video camera to tape the entire interview or a camera to take some photos.

The value of having photos and/or a video is that you can review your performance in the privacy of your home to see what you look like from the audience's perspective. You may be pleasantly surprised that you are better than you thought, or you might gain some outside perspective about your character that you hadn't noticed before. Having photos and a video of your character is a great way to stimulate your comedy imagination, because you are able to view yourself objectively.

Thanks to the amazing technology of the Internet, you have one more option available to you. Given that so many people are emailing files and creating profiles on community websites, why not put up your photos and share your video with friends. Ask for feedback, ideas, and suggestions. See what they say or what advice they may have. If you are wary of someone stealing your idea, then don't bother doing this; the anxiety will kill your joy. But, if you believe that your friends will be respectful and helpful, then take a chance and see what results you receive.

Another advantage of cyberspace is that you can receive help and advice from thousands of strangers. For example, if your character uses an Indian accent, perhaps you can find someone over the Internet to review your videotape and help you perfect your accent, gestures, or facial movements to make the character even more funny or authentic. The Internet places the world at your fingertips, so why not make use of the expertise that many people are willing to offer for free?

Step 7: Make Adjustments to Your Character

You've given birth to your character, clothed and accessorized him or her, presented the newborn to the world, and sought feedback. Now go back home and revisit your character in the peace and quiet of your own space. Consider what you might want to tweak, if anything. Did the character get the reaction you expected? Did the audience laugh when you thought they would? Were you completely comfortable being the character? Are you able to play your character repeatedly?

If your workshop audience provided feedback to you, was any of it helpful in targeting changes? Did their reactions gel with any of your own feelings?

Making adjustments is part and parcel of creating a strong and appealing comedy sketch character. Seldom does an actor hit the bull's eye in the first presentation. One reason is that you created the character and were guided by your sense of what might and might not work. You brought the character to life in the strongest way you knew how, but you cannot account for an audience's taste when you're new at comedy. It takes years to understand audiences and to develop your own personal sense of comedy. Many of the series regulars on *Saturday Night Live*, who have so brilliantly entertained us with their fabulous comedy sketch characters over the years, spent years of training at Second City in Chicago or the Groundlings in Los Angeles. I am sure they developed dozens of sketch characters over the years, yet we are familiar with only the ones that worked and will never know their flops.

The point is to keep working on your character. Take the time and don't give up on finding a better way to improve, enhance, and retool your character. Take him or her to a higher level. Solidify and embellish any traits that make the character clearer, more identifiable, more outrageous, and—of course— funnier! Always consider that even if you never get to use this character you are creating, the work you are doing will benefit you by stretching your comedy imagination.

Remember that in comedy, it's a rule of thumb to exaggerate character traits. Go as far as you can with them, rather than hold yourself back. If your character is from the south, come up with the strongest southern accent you can. If your character is a gravelly voiced smoker from New York, then talk as if you were chewing sand and dirt. You can always tone it down later. You don't want to play the character halfway; it's fine to be over the top.

Ironically, if you find yourself holding back on something, it is often indicative of the direction you should take. For instance, if a little voice in your head says you can't play a woman with a gravelly voice, then it's often a sign that you should do precisely that. Use that voice in your head as motivation to work harder.

Don't forget, when you make changes, to go back and update your Character Bio Page in your notebook and keep it current. The bio page is like the birth certificate for your character, and if it contains mistakes, you can get arrested for improper impersonation. OK, seriously, your bio page is necessary to keep track of your characters, so that you can continue to refine them.

Step 8: Have Your Character Write a Letter

Now that your character has gotten under your skin and become a new friend in your life, I highly recommend you get into your character and write a letter. What is the purpose of this letter? It is a great exercise in imagination building, and tremendously helpful for solidifying the thinking and language your character has in his or her mind. By writing a letter, you learn how to imitate your character's thought processes and word choices. This exercise is one more element in helping you anchor your character. As an added benefit, you could end up creating some hilarious ideas for your sketch comedy routine. Below are some topics you can choose, or you can—as always—create one of your own:

 A letter to the DMV complaining that you're waiting too long for your driver's license.
 A letter to your grocery store with suggestions for better service.
 A letter to your Congressman or Congresswoman asking for better parking on your street.

A letter to an umbrella company explaining that your umbrella broke in the last rainstorm and you want your money back.

Step 9: Take Your Character out in the Real World

You may be thinking, "Paul Ryan, are you crazy?" I'm not. I am completely serious. Yes, this step takes great courage, but it is truly worthwhile and useful to test your credibility. If you can walk out your door and have people believe your character, you've accomplished your goal—creating a character that appears real.

The best way to do this is to go to places you've never been before—and may never go again. Try a different part of your city or town, where no one knows you. You want to avoid anyone recognizing you and causing you to break character. You can go to a grocery store, a department store, a park, a gas station, a sporting event—or any place where you can interact with other people for a few minutes. Speak in your character's accent or dialect and wear your character's wardrobe. Observe how other people react toward you.

Depending on your character, it may also be useful to go to places authentic to your character. For example, if you are playing a southern character, find a country western bar. If you're playing an Italian or a Japanese person, go to your city's Italian or Japanese area. I am not suggesting you intentionally insult someone by pretending to be Japanese when you are clearly Caucasian. Be gracious and let people know you are working on a character and you'd like some help. However, if you do fit in, then go for it. Try to be as convincing as possible, so people completely believe who you are and where you are from.

This helps you to learn how to remain in character for long periods of time, no matter who is around. This is important if you plan to do professional work in TV or film, as shooting can take hours and you have to go in and out of character all day long. Appearing in public can also validate your character more than any work you do in a workshop. If the public accepts you, the audience will accept you as well. Tracey Ullman, a genius at creating brilliant authentic characters, has been known to stay in character all day long when she films.

Step 10: Begin Working Your Character into Scenes

You've come a long way to get to where you are. Your character is now a veritable living being that's been thoroughly tested, improved, rebuilt, and packaged. You have hopefully gotten the comedy seal of approval from yourself, your workshop, and perhaps from people in public.

So go back into your workshop class and begin working your character into the improvs you perform. Select a colleague who has also developed a character and do a scene together, where the two of you play your newly developed characters. Experiment with your character in a scene. For example, if your character is a quirky British tour guide, invent a scene where your character gives a tour of the Tower of London to a wealthy American industrialist who has hired you for the day. If you're playing a southern grocery clerk who works at the local Piggly Wiggly, you might want to set up a scene where he or she tries to help a customer pick out food for a special dinner. Use your comedy imagination to invent your scene and have fun!

Inhabit your character for a few days or weeks, as you perfect his or her appearance. Mix and match your character with ones created by other actors in your workshop to see if several of them can make beautiful music together. Maybe your character can end up dating another character. Or perhaps your character serves as a foil for another character. Be open to exploring many new possibilities. You never know what can happen through the synergy of several characters working together. Even if you decide to be a solo character, your continued work will help you to become more comfortable and versatile.

How to Know If Your Character Is Worth Keeping

It's possible that your character will hit the jackpot and propel you to fame, at least in your workshop. If so, that's great. Keep working the character until you decide you'd like to try your hand at doing the process again to see how much more comedy gold you can mine.

If you character was only so-so, don't fret. As I said before, many comedy characters don't survive for very long. They lose their oomph and pizzazz, or the actor simply gets bored with them. Sometimes you may feel that you want to abandon the character, despite all of the work you've put into it. Indeed, it can be very sad to give up on someone who has become close to you. Like breaking up with a partner, you may feel strange abandoning your character.

But be positive. The world is a big place, and you may decide at some point that it is best for you to go back to the drawing board to create and play another character. If so, look for something completely new and different. Open yourself up to other comedy opportunities that may come your way. Go back to observing the world, and you will likely find a new model to inspire your imagination.

Go back to step one and repeat the process again, step by step. Don't take any shortcuts just because you've been through it once. Each of these steps reinforces the prior one. Take your time and enjoy the work.

LEVEL III: INTERMEDIATE COMEDY EXERCISES, SERIES B

IF YOU'VE MADE IT TO THIS POINT IN THE BOOK, CONGRATULA-
tions! You are already demonstrating the level of dedication and perseverance needed to pursue a professional acting career. If you want to get
into TV, film, emcee work, or any other type of comedy acting, you have to
keep pushing yourself to learn more and more—even as others around you
fall by the wayside. You need to constantly challenge yourself to take on
tasks that seem difficult, unfamiliar, and possibly embarrassing.

The more you learn, the better you will be at your craft. This is more
than a cute saying—it's a truth worth remembering. The skills you master
today pave the way for the skills you will master tomorrow. Just as a toddler
must learn to crawl before walking, walk before running, and run before
bike riding, you have taken in a range of skills that are slowly setting you up
for your next level.

In this chapter, we are going to extend your range of skills to flesh out
your intermediate level of mastery. The categories we cover in this chapter
fall into six groups:

Sense Memory Development
Observational Powers
Spontaneity
Believability
Acting without Words
Incorporating Song into Your Comedy

Learning these skills will help you build a strong base that supports your
comedy talent and imagination. You don't want to go into the professional
world only to discover that you aren't equipped with all the basic skills and
experience that thousands of others already have. You just won't cut it if you
skimp on your training. So stick with it as you go through this chapter. Keep
challenging yourself as well as all of the participants in your group.

GROUP 1 EXERCISE: SENSE MEMORY

Sense memory refers to the ability to accurately recreate in your mind your
past sensory experiences. Having a powerful sense memory is essential to
comedy acting (and all acting) in two ways.

First, when you are playing a character, you need to be able to
experience the sensations that the character would be feeling in his or her
life. Reciting a character's lines of dialogue without truly seeing, hearing,
smelling, tasting, and touching what he or she has sensed is like telling

someone that you know what ice cream smells, feels, and tastes like without ever having seen it. You cannot be believable and real unless you can conjure up the real feelings of human senses as you play your characters and portray their lives.

Secondly, sense memory is what grounds you when you are acting out a character's life using props. Even with the best set design and most realistic props, acting is still a world of make believe. This means, for example, that when you appear onstage and smell a prop rose, you must be able to bring the real feelings of smelling a rose into your mind. In the momentary act of playing your part, you have to be able to make the audience see and believe in the rose.

When you put these two reasons together, you can see how sense memory fuels you as an actor. Whether you are working on stage or in a movie or TV show, you need to be able to feel the objects on the set and not take them for granted. When you play a character that is reminiscing about his mother and says, "She made the greatest spaghetti sauce in the world. It made our kitchen smell like the fanciest Italian restaurant," you need to be able to smell the spaghetti sauce in your mind as you say the line. Whatever you touch onstage and whatever line you say, you have to be able to activate your senses to make it real for you.

Sense memory work is so important to acting that many of the great elder statesmen of theater (such as the legendary acting coach Stella Adler) used to say that actors must practice sense memory work for two years before even thinking about auditioning for a role. Of course, these classical teachers did not live in our day and age, when people think they can study acting for three months and head out to claim their fame and fortune. In our quick-fix society, everyone thinks he or she can become a famous actor in a month or two. But just as you wouldn't go out and perform brain surgery after your first month of medical school, you shouldn't go out and audition after one month of sense memory work.

In my own comedy training, I was constantly taught to sharpen my senses as often as I could when I went anywhere or did anything. Sense memory work is something you have to do on a daily basis. You know how dentists will tell you to floss every day? Well, I am here to tell you to do your sense memory work every day.

There's another rationale that I always add into my discussions about the benefit of developing your sense memory. In my view, a lot of actors today seem to go onto a set relatively unconscious of what is happening around them. Many directors and casting people also confirm that some actors, because they become overly focused on their own lines, don't seem to pay attention to the other actors working with them.

Sense memory work can help you reduce, and even avoid, this problem because it trains you to be aware and keep your senses open. In other words, being in touch with your senses simply makes you more alive onstage. If you aim to become a professional actor, do as much sense memory work as you can when you are offstage.

SENSE MEMORY EXERCISE

You can practice sense memory any time you want because it doesn't require anyone else working with you. This is solo work, which you can do on the spur of the moment wherever you are. You might start off doing just a few minutes every day, as described below.

PEOPLE NEEDED: 1

DIRECTIONS: Sense memory exercises begin activating your senses by duplicating the sensation without the actual object. For example, rub your hand on a glass table. You may feel a smooth, polished, slightly cold surface. Keep rubbing your hand across the table, back and forth a few times, as you anchor the sensations deeply into your skin. Then, remove your hand. Can you feel the sensation of the glass on your skin? If not, keep rubbing your hand on the table until you can.

Here are five practices you can do on your own. Add to these any other sense memory you want to do. Each and every day, practice some type of sense memory work.

Feeling
Imagine petting a dog. Go and pet a real dog, then move your hand away and try to feel what it's like when the dog is not in front of you. Can you feel the sensation of the dog's fur? Bring that sensation to life. Try to fully develop your ability to feel the size of the dog, how far from the ground it is, and the tension in your lower arm as you stroke the dog. Should you ever need to stroke a dog when you are doing a scene, you can now make it appear believable.

Sound
Go to a busy street. Listen closely to the noises of pedestrians, cars, ambulances, fire engines, police sirens, etc. Then go to a quiet room and try to recreate all those sounds in your mind. If necessary, record the traffic with a tape recorder to remind yourself of the sounds.

Smell

Go to a florist shop and smell some flowers, or to a bakery, or even to a bus stop where you can sniff the diesel fumes. Go to a hot dog stand or a restaurant, where your favorite dishes are being prepared. Smell a dish that you dislike. Build your sense of smell so you can recreate the good, the bad, and the smelly.

Sight

Look at beautiful artwork and visually pleasing stimulus. Study the details so you can build your sense of sight. Find someone who has the silkiest skin, a chiseled nose, or a lot of freckles. Look at trees and their branches, swaying in the wind. Really study objects. Then walk away and try to visualize the object as fully as you can.

Taste

This is one of the more enjoyable parts of this exercise. Taste something delicious, like chocolate ice cream, and walk away, savoring the flavor. Challenge yourself. Taste things that are sour, bitter, hot, spicy, and bland. Build your sense of taste so you can recreate any flavor in your mouth.

GROUP 2 EXERCISE: OBSERVATION

Observation exercises go hand in hand with sense memory work, and focus on building your ability to see the details of objects—and not just vague outlines. The rationale for observation work is to help reinforce your sense memory, improving your ability to visualize objects with great clarity and specificity when you need to recall them onstage. Becoming highly observant is the method by which actors make their words ring with truth, not hollowness.

Many actors think that noticing minute details in objects will only serve to cloud their memory of the objects. On the contrary, studying a single detail in an object and then remembering it is one of the most powerful techniques for bringing an object clearly back into your memory. For example, if I want to bring a picture of my grandmother into my mind, I need only to think of a little Band-Aid in the right corner of her glasses. When I focus my memory on that one little detail, my grandmother springs to life in my mind.

Try this out for yourself. Go out and study an object, but focus on just one little detail. It may be a person or an object. Then go away and let some time pass. Then recall that one detail. See what I mean?

Being able to visualize a clear picture in your mind of any object will greatly improve your acting. By having the discipline to do this, you will really get something back from your acting. If your line of dialogue reads,

"You should have seen this guy, Jim, he works out three times a day," and you've been to your gym and focused on a guy with a six-pack stomach, believe me, you are going to recite that line of dialogue with more credibility than Arnold Schwarzenegger. Similarly, whenever you use a prop, you will have something behind your eyes. You have to have the senses awake, so that you are a living, aware human being.

OBSERVATION EXERCISE

Actors describe visual pictures all the time in their roles. But a good actor can truly see the picture behind the dialogue and make the audience believe that it is really there. That is what this exercise is all about.

Before doing this exercise, take some time to study an object in your living room, bedroom, or anywhere in your house.

PEOPLE NEEDED: 2

DIRECTIONS: Two actors go onstage and face the audience. One by one they tell the audience about something from one of the rooms in their homes. They describe the object to the other actor onstage as if they were describing it to an artist on the other end of a speakerphone. The actor should describe it in such detail, inch by inch, that an artist could simply draw it from the verbal description. The more the actor focuses on the details, the better the actor is able to see the object, even when nothing is there. For example, if you're describing a painting on your wall, you might say:

> "This picture is 24 inches wide by 24 inches long. A black frame that is four inches in width is all around it. Inside of the frame is a half-inch white strip of matting around the picture. There is a scratch on the glass in the lower left-hand corner."

The more details you can throw in, the more focused you will be at truly seeing the picture in your mind's eye. The goal of this exercise is for you to see what you need to see when you are onstage. This is extremely effective when you have to reminisce and make a person or object come to life for the audience. If a script mentions an Uncle Fred, for example, substitute an uncle from your own life, really see your uncle in your mind's eye. When the audience sees that you really see Uncle Fred, they will see him too.

GROUP 3 EXERCISES: SPONTANEITY

Many actors think the word spontaneity refers only to their ability to come up with snappy answers and jokes, but it's far more than that. In a larger sense, spontaneity is the gestalt of being in "the moment." When you are spontaneous, you are able to allow anything and everything to flow.

Spontaneous comedy actors bring freedom to their work. They are flexible, open-minded, uncensored, and in touch with their emotions. When they play a character, they can play the role deeply because they know how they feel inside, and that drives the credibility of their portrayal.

What does it take to infuse spontaneity into a comedy actor? First, you have to allow yourself to feel the flow of energy on the stage between you, other actors, the audience, and the stage area itself. The next time you are in front of an audience, stand and feel the energy that they emanate toward you. Each time you are onstage—either alone or with other actors—you are all exchanging a spontaneous energy.

Secondly, to learn to become fully spontaneous, you also have to release all of the pent-up emotions within you. In our world, far too many people tend to keep their feelings stuffed inside. They don't express themselves or their true emotions. The problem is that keeping your feelings suppressed may ultimately lead to problems like depression, disease, and dysfunction. Needless to say, it's hard to be spontaneous when you suffer from any of these! So if you are holding stuff in, begin releasing it. Do some introspection, talk to friends, or patch things up with family and friends. Whatever your problems are, begin to jettison them from your life. Do whatever it takes to free yourself, and let those emotions come to the surface! This will enable you to bring spontaneity more easily into your acting.

Finally, open yourself up to the world. Drop your prejudices, pet peeves, and phobias. Begin accepting the world for what it is—a huge, colorful, tasty circus that has lots of tents to explore. There is so much to learn, see, and do in the world. Go out and make it yours. Seek out joy in your life and pay attention to what you are feeling. Focus on how you can make the world feel better by knowing you. It's vital in your work as a comedy actor to learn to be spontaneous! If you love the world, it just may begin to love you back.

TELEPHONE CALLS

This exercise helps actors increase their ability to be completely sponta-neous. It builds listening skills and taps into observational powers and sense memory, since you need to visualize someone talking to someone on the phone. Phone work is a very important skill for actors to possess. There is hardly a TV show or movie where an actor doesn't have to pretend to talk on the telephone. So call on this exercise to help build your spontaneity and phone charm.

PEOPLE NEEDED: 2

SCENE: Two people talking on the phone.

DIRECTIONS: Two actors face the audience on opposite sides of the stage. They never look at each other, but strictly play to the audience. Each one holds a regular phone, a cell phone, or an imaginary one. The actors conduct a spontaneous conversation with each other. There is etiquette to phoning on camera. You should *never* hold the phone over your mouth, but rather place it so that the mouthpiece is just under your jaw. This allows the audience to see your entire face and expressions. Below are some suggestions for phone conversations:

> Telling an ex that you're getting married
> Telling a fellow actor you got a part in a TV show
> Ordering take-out from a restaurant
> Telling your boyfriend or girlfriend that you're moving in with him or her without asking
> A political candidate campaigning to a citizen
> A friend asking to borrow some money
> A husband calling a wife to tell her he bought a house without letting her see it
> A husband who's late for dinner and tells his wife he's lost
> A customer calling a department store with a complaint
> A citizen calling the police because his/her turtle is missing
> A relative calling another relative to get his or her opinion about a home shopping item
> A telemarketer calling a woman who has just started to have labor contractions
> A customer calling a store to complain about the price increase
> A patient calling a doctor trying to describe symptoms
> A patient calling a psychiatrist and giving lame excuses as to why they can't make the appointment

FILM TRANSLATION

This exercise is very challenging, because the spontaneity involves being able to talk in gibberish and to interpret someone else's gibberish. Robin Williams shines at this type of work, but you can, too, if you work hard to keep your mind and mouth loose. As you speak, don't worry about what your gibberish sounds like; focus only on staying in character and in the flow.

PEOPLE NEEDED: 4

SCENE: Two actors and two translators interpreting one another to the audience.

DIRECTIONS: Two actors (A and B) begin upstage while two actors (C and D) are downstage. Actors A and B are in a movie while Actors C and D are translators for the movie. Actor A speaks foreign-sounding gibberish for a bit, then Actor C, who has been watching, turns to the audience and immediately translates into English. Then, Actor B responds to Actor A, also in gibberish, as Actor D watches and immediately translates to the audience.

You can beef up the humor of this exercise with physical behavior and irony. For instance, if actor A speaks French-inspired gibberish and attempts to express love, he can act it out showing some romantic gestures. Actor C or D can then put a spin on it, interpreting that the actor A said, "I hate your guts." Then actor B must appropriately respond to what the translation is.

After the scene is over, it's important for the actors who translated to have the opportunity to play the gibberish role and visa versa. Some languages or accents you can base your gibberish on are:

Australian
British
French
Hebrew
Indian
Italian
Japanese
New York
Rapper
Scandinavian
Southern

WORKPLACE VENTING

This exercise allows three actors to work spontaneously in creating a scene together, sharing as much energy as they can. Because there are three actors, everyone must listen very carefully so that the participants don't overlap each other.

PEOPLE NEEDED: 3

SCENE: A group of coworkers taking a break.

DIRECTIONS: Three people come onstage from different directions. They congregate onstage as if they are at a lunchroom or the water cooler where they work. One of them begins to vent about their job, and then one-by-one, the other two join in. They reveal their frustrations and anger relating to whatever is happening in their jobs. Go ahead and make this a great bitch session. Take turns talking so that you follow the "Yes, and" improv commandment comedy rule, which states one person begins by telling a truth and the next person adds to it, followed by the next. Together you build a series of truths that form the comedy. Each actor must also work on seeing their environment in their mind's eye and physically represent their respective jobs. Some suggested work place scenarios are:

> Hair salon workers
> Celebrity personal assistants on a movie set
> Restaurant workers
> Hospital workers
> Gym employees
> People who work on a football team
> Actors working on a commercial
> Department store employees
> Bakery workers
> People working in a real estate office
> People working on a used car lot
> Hotel employees
> Psychics at a convention
> People working at a spa resort
> School employees
> People at a Tupperware convention
> Factory workers

YOU ARE THERE

This exercise is based on learning to portray someone from the past or present, using your knowledge of history or current events. The challenge is to bring your character to life with your own special spin. The spontaneity lies in the information you chose to work into your characterization. Since you have no time to research your character, go with the flow and use what you have available to you in the moment.

PEOPLE NEEDED: 3 or more

DIRECTIONS: One actor acts as an offstage interviewer, while two or more actors sit in chairs onstage. The interviewer announces that they will now portray either a modern or historical famous person or a fictional character from the list of pairs below. (The actors onstage don't know which characters they will portray until the interviewer announces them to the audience.)

The interviewer begins asking each actor opening questions that allow the actors to reveal their characterizations as best as they can. The actors must commit fully to their instincts and lose themselves in this new reality. They must actually believe they *are* the character.

Be sure to play off the other actor you are working with and feed off the questions the interviewer is asking you. Also, as you begin the improv, aim to find a hook, or theme, that you can develop with your partner. For instance, if you're playing Mr. and Mrs. Moses, and Moses talks about spending forty years in the desert, Mrs. Moses might add how she feels about him wandering for forty years, leaving her alone at home with the kids.

Some Present-Day Suggestions:
Britney Spears and her current partner
Jessica Simpson and her acting coach
George and Laura Bush
Bill, Hilary, and Chelsea Clinton
Madonna and her Kabbalah teacher
Aston Kutcher and Demi Moore
Jessie Jackson and his mistress
Whitney Houston and her ex Bobby Brown
Arnold Schwarzenegger and Maria Shriver
Queen Elizabeth and Prince Phillip
Prince Charles and Camilla
J-Lo and her ex-husbands
Catherine Zeta Jones and Michael Douglas
Michael Jackson, Latoya Jackson, Janet Jackson, and a plastic surgeon
Brad Pitt and Angelina Jolie
Nancy Kerrigan, Oksana Baiul, and Tanya Harding
Roseanne Barr and her former husbands
Martha Stewart and her former female prison-mates
Tom Cruise and Katie Holmes
Sylvester Stallone and his Shakespearean coach

Supermodels Tyra Banks, Lauren Hutton, Iman, and Naomi
    Campbell
Donald Trump, his wife Melania, and ex-wives Ivana and Marla
The Spice Girls
Elizabeth Taylor and her hairdresser Jose Eber
Richard Simmons and his female devotees who have lost weight
Hugh Hefner and his three girlfriends
The Dixie Chicks
M.C. Hammer, Ice-T, and Vanilla Ice
Ozzy and Sharon Osbourne
Judge Judy and two people she just tried on her TV show
Paris Hilton and Nicole Ritchie

Some Historical Suggestions:
Mr. and Mrs. Moses and their kids
George and Martha Washington
Mr. and Mrs. Ben Franklin
Mr. and Mrs. Paul Revere
Mr. and Mrs. Abe Lincoln
Albert Einstein and his wife
Thomas Jefferson and his mistress
Picasso and one of his protégés
Marie Antoinette and Louis XVI
Leonardo da Vinci and Mona Lisa
The two architects who built the Leaning Tower of Pisa
Caesar and Cleopatra
Christopher Columbus and Queen Isabella
Adam and Eve

Some Fictional and Cartoon Suggestions:
Jack and Jill
Hansel and Gretel
Cinderella and Prince Charming
Cinderella's wicked stepsisters
Mickey and Minnie Mouse
Popeye and Olive Oil
Sherlock Holmes and Dr. Watson

GROUP 4 EXERCISES: BELIEVABILITY

Comedy is about you being believable in a situation, whatever it may be, and allowing the comedy to come out of the situation. (As I've said many times already, sitcoms are funny because of the situations, but it's the actors being believable that makes the audience accept the situation—no matter how inane it is.) When you are believable, it affects everyone around you and deepens your acting.

One key to building your believability is to improve your listening habits. Make sure when you are onstage to always listen intently to what the other actors are saying. Stop the mind chatter that is usually in your head; you must completely throw yourself into the scene and *be* the character, truly listening to the other characters in the scene. You should have nothing else going on in your mind except your role. If you experiment with your listening skills, you will learn that the more you listen intently, the more energy and believability you will gain in your work.

Secondly, you can enhance believability by constantly stealing your gestures and mannerisms from real life. Use your sense memory and observational skills you practiced earlier to notice how people act and react in certain situations. For example, a reporter friend of mine who works for the show business publication *Daily Variety* was recently scheduled to interview a celebrity for an article she was writing. When she went to the publicist's office, where the celebrity was going to do the interview, the publicist stood up and shoved her hand within inches of the reporter's face, saying, "You have five minutes. Five! Do you hear me?" Her gesture was shocking and rude, but it was nevertheless a great gesture for an actor to use when he or she needs to portray someone who is angry or demanding.

Keep your eyes open for mannerisms and gestures you witness in your daily life. If you see something interesting, be sure to whip out your portable notebook and write it down, and then transfer it to your main Comedy Notebook for review later on.

In the exercises that follow in this section, you will have many opportunities to perform improvs that demand the utmost believability. Use all the comedy acting skills you've developed to this point to make yourself as credible as you can be.

DR. PHIL EXERCISE

People with problems are a rich arena to mine for your comedy gold, and Dr. Phil is living proof of how popular watching people talk about their problems is. This exercise combines these two elements and gives three actors a chance to work together on their believability. As with a TV sitcom, let the humor come from the situation you describe, not from you. Stay focused on being completely believable in your character.

PEOPLE NEEDED: 3

SCENE: A counselor giving advice to two people.

DIRECTIONS: One actor plays a counselor (like Dr. Phil) who talks to two other actors, who are portraying people with conflicts. The counselor assigns the other two actors the premise of the scene prior to the scene's beginning. The counselor is the straight man in the scene. Some suggested problems to portray are:

> I want to renew my vows, but he/she doesn't want to.
> I suspect my mate is having an affair, since he/she calls out names in his/her sleep.
> He/she's dumped me for the Federal Express man.
> He/she pays more attention to Fritzie, our dog!
> He/she's having desires to cross-dress.
> He/she's hooked on the talk shows from morning to night.
> He/she's spending all of our savings on home shopping networks.
> I need more sexual stimulation, and he/she needs less.
> He/she is the messiest roommate in the world.
> I don't understand—he/she talks, but he/she doesn't make any sense.
> My partner can't be real. He/she is always impersonating someone else.
> My partner is in love with himself/herself. He/she is constantly looking at himself/herself in the mirror.
> I'm married to the biggest hypochondriac in the world.
> My son/daughter can't get find someone to marry.
> He/she thinks soap operas are real. I don't know which character I'm coming home to.

TWO PEOPLE MEETING

This is another fun improv that requires you to work on your believability in an assigned comic situation.

PEOPLE NEEDED: 2

SCENE: Two people meeting.

DIRECTIONS: Two people enter from either side of the stage and meet in the middle. They enact one of the situations below. (Remember, they are coming from opposite directions.) Play your role as believably as you can. The audience knows the situation is a setup, but stay faithful to it. As in a TV sitcom, let the humor come out of the situation. Some suggested situations are:

Two people meet. One recognizes the other, but the other doesn't.
Two people meet and think they know each other, but actually have
    never met, so they can't figure out how they know each other.
Two people run into each other. One has been avoiding the other for
    years because he or she owes the other money.
Two unemployed actors meet and tell exaggerated lies about their careers.
A divorced couple meet, trying to act civilized, masking their mutual
    dislike.
Two former lovers meet and try to impress the other about their new
    relationships.
Two politicians running for the same office run into each other.
Two former mothers-in-law meet after the kids have divorced.
A sergeant and private, who were in the army together years ago, meet up.
    The private is now an important man; the sergeant is not doing much.
A star and a fan meet, and the fan goes wild.

GOING BACKSTAGE

Going backstage after a performance is a rich area to mine for comedy, and this exercise does exactly that. The humor comes out of the fact that going backstage can be embarrassing to either the actor who has just finished the performance or to the guests who saw the performance—or to both. This exercise offers a variety of situations to play, while also building your believability. At the risk of sounding like a broken record, let me remind you to let the comedy come out of the situation.

PEOPLE NEEDED: 2 or more

SCENE: Two people are discussing a situation backstage.

DIRECTIONS: Select one of the situations below and enact it.

Suggested Situations:

Two agents go backstage after they see their client in a terrible performance. The first two-thirds of the scene is about beating around
the bush before the ending, in which they drop the bomb that they
are letting the client go.

A mother and father from Iowa come to see their daughter or son in
an off-off Broadway play, only to discover that their child was naked
in the second act. As they come backstage, the father tries to console
the mother who is crying hysterically. The child responds, "Please,
Mom and Dad, I'm twenty-one years old." You take it from there.

A redneck from the south, Billy Bo Bob, has gone to see his best
friend performing in a Shakespearean play, or any sophisticated play.
He goes backstage to congratulate his friend, but then asks lots of
dumb questions indicating that he had no idea what the play was
about. Given that there are other actors in the dressing room, the
actor is embarrassed by his southern friend.

A columnist is interviewing an actor backstage after a show. A third
actor in the dressing room sees this as an opportunity to chime in
and try to steal the limelight.

A director goes backstage to give notes to two actors. One of the
actors' ego is so inflated that he or she can't accept any of the suggestions, no matter how good they are. The other actor tries to help, but
gets mixed up in the crossfire. Let a heated argument ensue, and
may the best man or woman win!

An ex-lover who dumped the actor now sees the actor as desirable,
and goes backstage to test the waters now that the actor is famous
and successful.

A friend, who is owed $1,000 by his or her recently successful actor-
friend, goes backstage to collect the money that is owed.

A dear high school friend goes backstage to ask his or her actor-
friend if they can spend some time together. But the actor is now
snooty, acting as if he or she is a gigantic star.

SLIDE SHOW FROM HELL

This is an opportunity for four actors to work together, building a relationship in a believable situation. The exercise also develops visualization skills, because you have to portray to the audience what you see on an imaginary screen during the slide show.

PEOPLE NEEDED: 4

SCENE: Two couples watching a slide show.

DIRECTIONS: One couple is onstage, excited at having their friends come over to view slides of their latest adventure. The second couple enter. The action begins as the first couple invites the second couple to watch the slide show. The actors face the audience, playing out front, while watching the slide presentation. One of the hosts can make a clicking sound, as if they're hitting a button to move through the slides.

The second couple can choose to react in a myriad of ways to the endless presentation. They can be bored, more excited than the hosts, make comments about weird slides, or you might have the two women get excited, while the men are bored. Don't decide this in advance, but let the improv proceed with spontaneity. Some suggested events/adventures for the slide show are:

Bar Mitzvah/Bat Mitzvah
Birth of Their Child
Camping Trip
Family Christmas
High School Reunion
Liposuction Operation
Spiritual Retreat
Surprise Birthday Party
Vacation
Wedding

GROUP 5 EXERCISES: ACTING WITHOUT WORDS

Actors often depend completely on words to show their talent. But learning to act without words is a critical skill, because it builds your ability to express emotions without relying on any words to convey your feelings. When you don't have words, you have to use your body and face to tell the audience what is going on inside you. Comedy, specifically, compels you to use physical behavior to incite humor.

Three of the greatest actors in this arena were Buster Keaton, Harold Lloyd, and Charlie Chaplin. Given that their acting careers occurred during the silent movie era (though Chaplin later moved into talkies), they were forced to learn how to show comedy without the use of words. If you've never seen a Keaton, Lloyd, or Chaplin movie, rush out and rent a few. Their facial expressions, body movements, physical stunts, and comedic timing make these actors among the greatest comedic talents in the history of film.

One of the keys to acting without words stems directly from your believability. As I tell my students, you must stay in your role completely when you have no words. If you have a real thought, the audience will see that thought.

The two exercises in this group will challenge you to new heights in your comedy acting. Try your best to perform the improvs without resorting to words. Convey to your audience whatever you are thinking using only your body and face.

ACTING OUT AN EMOTION

This is a simple, straightforward exercise in which you must show feelings on command without using any words. You may use sounds, but no language.

PEOPLE NEEDED: 3

SCENE: Two actors onstage physically acting out emotions.

DIRECTIONS: Two or more actors are onstage, facing out front, while another actor offstage calls out the changes. The narrator yells out one emotion from the list below, and both actors must then physically act out the emotion immediately. The offstage person then calls on one person at a time, so they can make appropriate sounds to the emotion. When the participants complete the first emotion, the narrator moves on to the next emotion. Some suggested emotions are:

Angry
Cheerful
Disappointed
Euphoric
Excited

Expectant
Frustrated
Happy
Hurt
Loving
Sad
Shocked
Tearful
Thrilled
Worried

ANNOYING HABITS

This improv between two actors is performed completely in silence. All the humor in the exercise must come from the actors' movements and timing.

PEOPLE NEEDED: 2

DIRECTIONS: One actor is sitting in a movie theater, watching a film and thoroughly enjoying it. An empty chair is next to that actor. The second actor enters and takes the empty seat. The first actor can react in any way he or she wants. Then, as the second actor begins watching the movie, he or she slowly portrays an annoying habit from the list below. The habit starts subtly, but builds to the point of complete interference with the first actor's enjoyment of the movie. The first actor never looks at the actor with the rude habit, but slowly gets infuriated by the annoyance. The first actor's goal is show the audience what he or she in thinking without using any words or sounds. The audience must see the actor transition from enjoyment to a subtle nervous breakdown by the end. Some suggested habits for the second actor are:

Humming
Foot tapping
Sneezing
Lint picking
Snoozing
Making little grunts
Talking to him or herself
Trying to clear nasal passages
Finger snapping
Coughing

Gawking

Playing with a noisy candy wrapper

GROUP 6 EXERCISE: INCORPORATING SONG INTO COMEDY

Are you afraid of singing? Do you think you have a bad singing voice? Well, I have to tell you that it doesn't matter; you need to learn how to use song in your comedy for several good reasons.

First, singing breaks down the last of any die-hard inhibitions you may have about being onstage. Singing forces you to get in touch with your inner child, where you completely accept yourself no matter how silly or stupid you may look and sound to others. Children don't worry about what they sound like when they sing; they're not concerned with whether they are on key or whether their tempo is right. They simply sing to their hearts' content. So get yourself back to the innocence you had as a child and infuse your comedy acting with a song.

Another value to singing is that it can inspire you comedically. Whether you were told not to sing or you took on negative thoughts about your singing, it's likely that you have closed down a section of the "ham" in you that allows you to be playful. By opening yourself to singing, you can begin to free your "ham-self" at a very deep level.

A third benefit of allowing yourself to sing is that it provides an energy boost. If you've ever seen a Broadway musical, you know that musical theater actors must maintain an enormous amount of energy day in and day out. In my view, this happens because they sing and dance throughout their performances, which strengthens their stamina, rather than depleting it.

Why might you need to have so much energy as a comedy actor? Believe it or not, working on TV sitcoms demands high energy and the ability to maintain it for long periods of time. TV sitcoms often take hours to shoot, and, like a musical, you must be able to get into character without losing any energy.

Finally, another reason to allow yourself the freedom to sing is that no matter what your voice sounds like, it offers yet another style of comedy for you to work in. Many comedy actors, like Will Ferrell who starred in the film version of the musical *The Producers*, accept roles in productions that require singing to stretch and show their range.

The exercise below challenges you to sing during the entire improv. Allow yourself to fully experience the joy of singing. Forget any worry you may have about your voice. Even if you are tone-deaf, let yourself be free as a bird singing its head off.

SINGING STORY

In this exercise, four actors must tell a story in song. What's fun about this improv is the range of voices you will get, depending on the team of actors onstage.

PEOPLE NEEDED: 3 or 4

DIRECTIONS: Three or four actors are onstage playing out to the audience. An offstage narrator gives them a topic or theme from the list below. Begin the improv with the actors talking. The first actor starts off telling a story with a lot of energy. The second actor picks it up and moves the story along. Each subsequent actor must continue in the same way by progressing the story with words only.

When the first actor begins the second round, he or she must now sing to continue telling the story, using any melody, whether copied from another song or completely made up. Be free to pull from a variety of musical styles, such as country western, opera, blues, Broadway, pop, rock, jazz, scatting, rap, hip-hop, Spanish folklore, or lullabies for kids. The second actor continues in song, using the previous melody, or any style he or she chooses.

For the third round, all actors will continue singing; but this time, as the last person wraps up the story, he or she must sing one line, and the others must immediately adopt it and sing along in chorus.

As a real challenge, while singing the final line, the last person can initiate a dance step that the others must also follow. Together, you will build to a show-stopping finale. Try to achieve the look of a closing number in a show you've been rehearsing for months. Some suggested topics are:

What's Happening on Television
Fashion around the World
How to Shop for Bargains
The Latest on Madonna
The History of the World
Our Best Presidents
How to Be a Great Parent
The Meaning of Life
What's Happening in the Music Scene
How to Make Money
How to Be in the Best Shape of Your Life

TAKING IMPROV INTO THE WRITTEN SCENE

NOW THAT YOU HAVE DEVELOPED A LEVEL OF IMPROV FREEDOM, it's time to transfer that talent into comedy scene work. As opposed to improv, the words and dialogue are not written by you spontaneously, but are written by other comedy writers. I have a very specific way of dealing with this aspect of comedy acting.

What Type of Scenes to Do

If you are new to reading scenes, I recommend that you look for scenes that are two to three minutes in length. There are dozens of anthologies of comedic scenes that you can buy, and Neil Simon is truly one of the best. You will benefit greatly by taking the time to read well-written scenes. It isn't something you do once or twice. If you don't work at it, it's difficult to grow as an actor, and you'll impede your progress. I know many people who only study improv, and when they go to read for a part, they don't get it because they haven't practiced what this chapter is all about.

PHASE 1: PREPARING THE SCENE BY YOURSELF

First, read the scene for enjoyment, as if you're reading an article in *People* magazine. Appreciate the writer's style, words, and character development. A lot of actors have the habit of immediately wanting to memorize or recite the lines as they read the material for the very first time. Actors are not robots. Comprehension is the first order of the day. You need to get the lay of the land before going in for the kill.

If you have the entire play, TV sitcom script, or screenplay, read *all* of it in order to get an overview of the entire plot. This way, you can see how each individual scene plays into the plot. Find out what happens before and after your scene, as well as how your character evolves. Get out of the quick fix mentality. Refrain from memorizing it and learning it the first time you read it through. Stay in neutral and just see from reading the material what pops off the page at you.

Next, read the scene a second time, being much more attentive. Become a detective; give the writing an opportunity to reveal its clues as to what exactly is going on. Ask yourself questions about what's happening in the scene, what the author is trying to express, and what your character is trying to achieve. Keep reading it over until you feel that you fully understand the scene. You can't play the scene unless you fully understand it.

Write down a concise summary of the scene. Understanding the truth of the scene is critical. It's just not good enough to think it. Write down a laser-sharp, concise summary of the scene and a statement about its comedy essence. Don't go on and on for days with a lot of paragraphs. Try to boil it down to two sentences at the most.

For example, let's say you are working on the "Johnny and Wilma" scene from the play *Lovers and Other Strangers*, written by Renee Taylor and Joe Bologna (it was later turned into a movie). You might write down something like this for your first pass:

> This scene takes place in a bedroom. The wife is furious that her husband has not made the advances she wants. It turns into a full-blown marital argument. The humor of the scene is that we have a reversal of the stereotypical male-female demands for making love. She acts like a prosecuting attorney or angry truck-driver, demanding that her husband have sex with her. He plays the not-tonight-dear role, causing her to escalate her frustration.

Next, reduce your statement to the real essence. Aim to boil it down to only one or two sentences. For example, we might take the above and laser it to the following:

> A volcanic argument erupts when the marital roles reverse, and a wife, acting like a truck driver, demands sex from her unwilling and tired husband. The conversation goes from bad to worse, as they begin dragging out every piece of minutiae about their marriage and pressing each other's buttons in a valiant effort to win the argument.

Don't worry if your statement is not perfect. You can change it or add to it as you develop the scene; but for now, put something down that reflects your current understanding.

PHASE 2: WORK WITH YOUR PARTNER TO PREPARE THE SCENE

Get genuinely enthused about the scene. You can't do a scene if you don't believe in its humor, and you can't play it well unless you are completely tuned into the part. Get connected to the scene, and buy into it 100 percent. You can do this in several ways. If you're working with a partner, the two of you might share your individual statements, interpreting the story to each other. It has to be like a telling a joke and believing it's funny. Did you ever try to tell a joke that you didn't think is funny? It doesn't work. Another way to share with each other is to imagine that you are pitching the scene to a producer, who might put some money up to produce the material. The point of this role-playing is to get excited and committed to the scene.

Find something in your own life that personalizes the scene. Ask yourself this question: What does this remind me of in my own life? This is called personalization, a critical step in bringing yourself into the work. Personalizing allows you to bring your own life experiences into the role that relates to something that happens in the scene. For example, the scene from *Lovers and Other Strangers* might remind you of a specific knock-down, dragged-out fight that you had with your significant other. Find a specific event, not just a general situation that happened in your life. If you can't, then find an argument that you maybe had with a neighbor, a friend, or the grocery store clerk. Don't bother asking friends to help. You want to find something in your own life—not theirs. Also, don't begin spending time thinking of an event or feeling that represents the other character. That won't help, either. For example, if you're playing the male role in a scene, don't think about a story that pertains to the female role. Focus on something in your own life.

Role-play your personalization. Describe to your acting partner the personality of the person you are envisioning in your role-play. Give him or her the circumstances of the argument you had with the person in your life. If the person was cocky, tyrannical, or moody, tell your acting partner so that he or she can bring the person to life for you. This will allow you to bring yourself into the scene. Once you've shared this information, do a one-minute improvisation with your acting partner. Your goal is to anchor the emotion and bring you into the scene, which will enable you to relate to the dialogue more easily.

Right after you role-play, sit down with your acting partner and talk about the scene. Identify the action you are trying to accomplish. Find some action words, or better, an action verb to inspire you. This technique is called the "Major Overriding Action." Ask yourself if your character is manipulating, coercing, buttering up, extracting information, or venting frustration at the other person. Targeting this as a single action helps you to be specific in your approach to the role and the scene.

After finding a verb that works for you, write it down. If you decide your action verb is "to persuade," write "My action is to persuade a stubborn mule." If your verb is "to manipulate," you might come up with "My action is to manipulate my controlling mother."

This extra characterization at the end of the sentence gives you an attitude toward your acting partner. Another advantage of adding these details is to keep your mind focused on your work when you finally act out the scene. There will be less of a chance that your mind will drift.

Your choice is your talent! You must find the personalization and the action verb that pays the most gold for you. Don't settle for something trivial. For example, if you were performing the scene above, you may not relate to an argument with a spouse over sex, but certainly you've had huge arguments with someone who has pressed your buttons. So be sure you think about the most explosive situation that will feed you the most. I've had actors in my studio who tell me, "Well, I don't really argue with anyone, so I'm not sure how to do this scene." I tell them if they're breathing (and they are), they've had some sort of conflict in their life. If you are having difficulty, go to your Comedy Notebook and check your Self-Inventory lists and see if you've written down something related to the scene you are working on. Support your acting partner as well. Do for your partner what you did for yourself. Don't let your partner coast. Get him or her to dig as well.

PHASE 3: REHEARSING THE SCENE WITH YOUR PARTNER

You are now ready to play the scene. The several steps below will guide you to playing the scene correctly.

Step 1: Read the scene with your partner while sitting down, script in hand and acting it out. This is the first time you will be reading the lines from the script. Do *not* focus on memorizing the lines now. Do not stand up or follow any stage directions at this point. Simply play the scene while seated with the script held in front of you, not on the table. You are sitting down, but hold the script out so you can see your partner easily. You can be sitting in two chairs facing each other or side-by-side, however you want. Keep some tension in your wrist so you can hold your script in place. I give my students this direction all the time, and I'm always amazed how many times they drop their arm and put the audition "sides" on their lap. Don't do that. Get into the habit of holding the scene in front of your eyes, in front of your chest, so you can look at your partner as he or she reads.

The important thing in this particular reading is that when your partner speaks his or her lines of dialogue, you must look at them so you can receive their energy. Look down at your script only when you are reading your own lines. Keep your thumb on your lines, slowly moving it down as the scene progresses so you don't lose your place. By looking at the other person, you open yourself to being affected by what he or she says. If you sit there and look down at the lines while your partner is reading, you close yourself off to reacting to what is said. There are many parts of the brain that are activated when you read and these skills are enhanced the more you do it.

Step 2: Read the scene again to allow a flow. This time, your objective is to become more comfortable with the scene. This time really allow your partner to affect you at a deeper level.

Step 3: Break apart the scene to identify the beats and minor actions. Read the scene a third time with your partner with an eye to noticing where it shifts. Most scenes are not one long flowing piece but have changes, called beats, where there are variations in the scene. This could be a change of physical action, a subtle emotional change in the character, a decision the character makes, a change of topic in the discussion, or a change in pacing. Just as in life, people are inconsistent and unpredictable.

Some beats are obvious, because the writer clearly put them in there. Other beats are your own choice—they are where you as an actor want to distinguish one piece of the scene from another using your own creativity.

Your job is to discover or create these beats and divide the scene up. This means that as you read this scene, you and your partner need to be in character when you read, and go out of character as you analyze the scene and talk about the beats. The two of you work together to identify and agree on the beats that you'd like to use to give the scene nuance.

Step 4: Assign each beat its own action verb. Although you gave the entire scene an overriding major action verb in the preparatory phase, now you want to distinguish the minor beats of the scene with an action verb. That's why it's important to study the action sheets I gave you in Chapter 3 so that your mind is more attuned to the wide range of verbs that create possible nuances. This is what allows you to create variety in the scene so you're not stuck in one-note acting.

As you learn the scene, you want to use all these nuances so they will translate to your audience. For example, let's say you're doing a scene with a female character trying to get her resistant boyfriend to go with her on a vacation. While the overriding action of this scene might be "to persuade this stubborn mule," you may feel that the scene has the following four beats: in beat #1, you might be "hinting," and in beat #2, you might be "confronting," and in beat #3, you might be "enticing" and in the final beat, you might be "seducing." With these four beats, you've now delineated the scene with subtleties that add more interest and depth.

It's like you're taking the scene on a roller-coaster ride, with ups and downs and upside downs that give it movement and a sense of unpredictability in the work. You have to consider that the writer did not aim to create a flat one-dimensional scene, and now you as the actor must avoid that, too, in interpreting the scene.

For example, in a scene from *Butterflies are Free* (a movie I was in), the blind character Don Baker says to the character Jill Tanner, "I've always wanted to know what I look like." She replies, "Really cute." He then says, "Really?" Now, I've had a lot of students in my classes who simply say the word and think that's enough. They're not putting in the sub-text, how Don must feel about being told that he is really cute, when he's never seen himself in a mirror. You can't act the word "really" if you don't explore what could be underneath it.

Step 5: Discover your character's traits and the clues the lines give you.

Now that you have been breaking the scene apart, you are becoming familiar with what traits your character possesses—the way he or she behaves. You might notice, for example, that your character is sensitive, defensive, combative, or has a good sense of humor. Or you notice character traits in your partner that you want to play off. This is why it is beneficial to do your self-inventory lists, so you are aware of those elements and can personalize them.

You also want to look closely at your lines to see what clues they are giving you about your character and your partner. You can often discover hidden meanings and agendas that you may have not yet picked up on about your character.

Consider this example. In Neil Simon's play, *The Prisoner of Second Avenue* (which became a movie starring the late comedy legends Jack Lemmon and Anne Bancroft), there is a particularly wonderful comedic scene where the character Mel comes home to his wife Edna to find out they've been robbed. Unbeknownst to Mel, Edna hadn't been able to find her keys and had left the apartment unlocked when she went shopping. When she came back, she discovered the apartment had been ransacked. Mel then comes home and can't figure out how they got ransacked. Edna tells him that she was out shopping for a while, insisting that she was only gone five minutes. She's lying and Mel starts to get very suspicious.

This is an example of where it's the actor's job to be perceptive about the dialogue and deeply understand the lines. If you were pulling the scene apart, you would notice that Edna says three times, "I was only gone five minutes." When Mel hears this, he begins challenging her, which affects how you would need to play the next part of your scene. Similarly, when Edna senses that Mel doesn't believe her, she begins feigning shortness of breath, which affects how you need to play her next part of the scene.

This struggle and conflict is what creates the comedy and you and your partner must discover this in the lines. There is no substitute for getting underneath the words before you say them.

Step 6: Read the scene yet again, with your understanding of the major beats, the minor beats, your character traits, and your relationship with each other.

You've done a huge amount of preparation and you are both very knowledgeable about the scene and your characters, your objectives, where you're going, the conflicts, timing elements, and pacing. You have a sense of the beginning, middle, and end of the scene.

Now you are ready to read it again, and this time, your goal is to allow all the *subtext* to come to life. When we say subtext, we are referring to what is going on below (sub) the text, which is what's underneath the lines of dialogue. The subtext is what you've been discovering in all the work you've done in all the steps of your preparation that you've taken up to this point. It's the underbelly of the scene, e.g., the character's motivations, unsaid thoughts, goals, background, and so on.

It's just as in your own life: when you're talking to someone, you don't verbalize everything. Your mind has many thoughts and feelings that remain unsaid. It's like those bubbles you see in comic strips representing thoughts that characters have and never say. The same is true for any scene you act, and this is why you've done so much preparation to understand the subtext.

Think of your partner and yourself as architects who have created a blueprint from which you can work. Like a blueprint, you have looked at your characters from the top, side, and bottom, and you've created all the details that make up the foundation of the scene.

By the way, you still have not memorized the scene, but it's likely that you've become very familiar with the dialogue and the words are jumping off the page into your mind without much effort. When I coach people who go off and memorize the scene first, I find that they are locked into delivering their lines in a completely monotonous, flat, one-note way. That's why I say: don't memorize the scene until you are further along in the process.

TAKING A BREAK

In Phase 1, you worked alone according to your own schedule. In Phases 2 and 3, you have been working with your partner and you might wonder how much you should attempt to do in a single day. The answer is up to you. You might want to complete all of Phases 2 and 3 in one sitting, or perhaps you might want to do Phase 2 one day, then Phase 3 another day. I do recommend that you take a break—for a few hours or overnight—between Phases 3 and 4 so you can let your creativity incubate and rejuvenate. A little break can benefit your mind and help you and your partner approach your work in a fresh way. Sure, if you have an audition in a few hours and need to get ready, then stay with it, but otherwise, take a break.

PHASE 4: PUT THE SCENE ON ITS FEET

Step 1: Rehearse the scene, standing up, back to back. I recommend that the first step you and your partner take when coming back after your break is to act out the scene in character, but standing back to back. This teaches the two of you to listen to each other in a new way and hear what you might not have heard because you have been focusing on looking at each other. It is really an exercise in becoming closely attuned to what each of you is really saying. An interesting approach is to pay more attention to the other person than yourself. It makes for more textured acting, because actors tend to focus so much on themselves that they stop listening. This exercise really gets you to listen to your voices, hearing every tonal quality.

Step 2: Block the Scene. In this step, you are now ready to stand on your feet and add movement, known as *blocking*. Blocking refers to the various physical actions of a scene, such as characters going from one room to another, or from one piece of furniture to another. If you don't know already know stage directions, here is a brief primer: Blocking is always done from the point of view of the actor onstage, looking out at the audience. Thus, stage right refers to the actor taking a step to his right; stage left refers to the actor taking a step to his left. If the actor moves closer to the audience, it is called moving downstage. Moving away from the audience is called moving upstage.

One of the sacred rules of blocking is that characters must have motivation to move anywhere on the stage. This means that when you block a scene, you need to assign each movement according to an impulse the actor would feel. Sometimes this might be associated with a line of dialogue the actors says, but other times, it is associated with a reaction the actor has to what another character says. Above all, movement is not random. The purpose of it is to open up the scene, and add some visual variety.

This is not to say that every scene must have a lot of movement. You can overdo it. Some scenes may already have some blocking written into them by the author. The director's job is to figure out all the blocking or to supplement whatever blocking has not been supplied by the writer. In TV sitcoms, some directors will allow the actors to walk around the set and discover their own blocking, while other directors want to control the blocking every step of the way.

If you're blocking a scene with your partner, and you don't have a director, the two of you must block it together. See what naturally flows as you go through the scene. Only move when you feel it's necessary. If you feel like moving, look at it as experimentation, an exploration, without cementing it right away. Allow your blocking to change as you go through the entire scene, because every movement is influenced by the preceding and subsequent movements. You don't want to have a scene that has characters always moving in the exact same pattern monotonously.

Step 3: Rehearse the scene with your blocking as many times as you need.

This is the point of a rehearsal where you are completely in character and doing the scene for real, but without an audience. Let yourselves rehearse as much as you need. There are several goals in rehearsing.

The more you rehearse, the less you need to look at your script, because the words become part of you through the repetition. For many actors, this is a more natural way to learn lines than rote memorization. You still may need to study your lines for memorization, but the more you learn them in rehearsal, the more natural your performance will be.

The more you rehearse, the more you will identify where the comedy timing lies. The rehearsal process allows you the opportunity to perfect the timing. Note: any comedy actor will tell you that you can never predict where the audience will laugh. Audiences have been known to laugh at lines that actors never considered funny. So keep in mind that whatever you discover in the comedy timing now, you must be flexible when you finally have an audience.

Rehearsing helps you anchor your performance. The more you go through your scene, the more comfortable you will feel about it. This way you don't need to worry about remembering your lines, blocking, where you are going, where the changes are, and all the shifts. You eliminate the guesswork.

The irony of rigorous structured rehearsal is the way it allows greater freedom in performance. That freedom can often lead to greater creativity. With freedom comes imagination and your creative juices can really start to flow. Even after all the work you've done up to this point, you may suddenly come up with a new idea that seems to work better. Allow yourself to be open and free to the new creativity that bubbles up as you rehearse. These are moments when genius often comes through.

Step 4: Taking Your Work and Putting It in Front of Other People

When you feel you are ready, invite a few people to watch your work. You don't need a big audience, as this is just scene work. Audiences serve many purposes:

First, having an audience will help you see where the laughs are. As I said before, it's hard to predict where audiences will laugh and for how long—and in fact, each performance will be different. This is why actors who do Broadway shows and long theater runs say each audience has its own personality, and gives them something new each performance.

An audience also helps you confirm that you've done the scene in the best way. You may notice that the audience doesn't react in the way you expected, and it could be because your action was unclear or you didn't set up the punch line clearly enough. If desired, you can ask the rehearsal audience for feedback at the end of the performance. You might even take their notes and adapt them into your performance, doing the scene again in front of them.

Finally, needless to say, having an audience is the final payoff for most actors. It's the performance that gives you the high and refuels your motivation to keep acting and working on your skills. It's what helps you maintain the dream.

Tips about the World of Comedy Acting

Consider each sentence in a scene as a separate thought. Many actors, when they have several lines in a row, have a tendency to run their lines together as one thought and one feeling. But in real life, we don't know what we are going to say next. I may take a pause to gather my thoughts. I may be in a tirade and have a slew of thoughts come out like a machine gun. It all depends. The lines give you the clues, so pay attention to every line, and don't feel like you have to spill them out all at once.

Recognize that a lot of comedy scripts are based on a pattern of set-ups and punch lines. The setup can be one line, or several lines of dialogue between the characters, followed by the punch line.

It's not always a given that one character is the straight man, while the other is the comedian. The characters can often change roles in the course of a scene, so don't assume that your part is or is not the straight man part.

Sometimes playing in opposite ways to what's written can be very effective. For example, instead of being blatantly inquisitive and judgmental, you might pretend to be friendly and charming. A good example of this is in the movie *When Harry Met Sally*, where Meg Ryan plays out the famous orgasm scene in the restaurant. Rather than be judgmental of Billy Crystal's character on why he has so many girlfriends and asking accusingly "What do you do with these women," she pretends to be non-judgmental and curious. She leads him into answering honestly by acting like a good friend. Once he has confessed to sleeping with a lot of women and leaving them early in the morning, she nails him when she says, "That's disgusting."

The more material you read, the more you will learn how to detect nuances and possibilities. Some scenes are broad comedy, meaning that the characters are playing over the top, larger than life. *Seinfeld, Will & Grace*, and *Friends* are examples of broad comedy. Other shows are subtle comedies like *Frasier* or *The Bob Newhart Show*, which use more irony and sophistication in their writing.

A NOTE ABOUT PREPARING AND PERFORMING COMEDY MONOLOGUES

It's a must to learn to do both scenes and monologues, which are sometimes required in auditions. There are several kinds. A character may deliver a long speech within the context of a scene with other characters. That's one type of monologue. Or a character may have a long speech while onstage alone—that's another type of monologue. Both are important to undertake. No matter which type you are doing, in an audition you should always perform the monologue straight out front.

When preparing a monologue, you must go through all the steps that we've covered in this chapter. The only difference is that you won't have a partner to share ideas or rehearse with. However, if your monologue is from a play that has two characters in your scene, you still want to examine the other character and determine the major overriding action and the beats of the scene so you can understand the complete context of your monologue.

Some monologues also contain lines that "break the fourth wall," meaning the character unhooks from the person he was talking to and talks directly to the audience.

When you perform a monologue, your goal is to bring the person to whom your character is talking to life. This is where your sense memory and observation comes in. You need to be able to conjure up an image of the person to whom you are speaking.

Developing Your Scene Work

You can never do enough scenes. I believe that all actors need to work on scenes for years, even if they land parts and become famous. Scenes help you remain fresh and fertile. Great actors like Al Pacino and Robert De Niro are constantly studying their craft. Many actors also do live stage, Broadway, and summer stock to keep their acting tools sharpened.

If you intend to go after an agent, you want to have at least two acting scenes with different partners available at a moment's notice. If you have only one scene and your acting partner is away, you're cooked.

In addition, you want to have two comedy monologues available that are different; one may work in an agent's office, while the other works in a theater audition.

I'll address more details about preparing for auditions in Chapter 9.

GOOD COMEDY SCENE SUGGESTIONS

Some comedies that have superb acting scenes to work on are:

Prisoner of Second Avenue by Neil Simon
Lovers and Other Strangers by Renee Taylor and Joseph Bologna
Butterflies Are Free by Leonard Gershe
Barefoot in the Park by Neil Simon
The Chinese and Dr. Fish by Murray Schisgal
Beyond Therapy by Christopher Durang
The Odd Couple by Neil Simon (there's a version for two men and one
    for two women)
Plaza Suite by Neil Simon
Brighton Beach Memoirs by Neil Simon
Play It Again, Sam by Woody Allen
California Suite by Neil Simon
Biloxi Blues by Neil Simon

Enter Laughing by Carl Reiner
The Sisters Rosensweig by Wendy Wasserstein
Lobby Hero by Kenneth Lonergan
The Heidi Chronicles by Wendy Wasserstein
Well by Lisa Kron
Picasso at the Lapin Agile by Steve Martin
It Had to Be You by Renee Taylor and Joseph Bologna

FINAL THOUGHTS ON SCENE WORK

Just to drive it home one more time: resist memorizing the dialogue outside of rehearsal. It's the kiss of death. The lines will sink in as you are dissecting the material. And they will enter your mind with more truth and reality because you will comprehend where they are coming from.

Another trap actors tend to fall into is to say each line in a sequence the same way. You want to make sure that you think about each and every word you utter. You've got to connect with what's going on in your head as you're saying the line. At the end of each line is the termination of a thought. The next line is the beginning of a new thought. That's the way we talk in real life. We don't want to say everything the same way or with what the entertainment industry calls a "one-note approach." Variety is the spice of life—and an essential quality in performing a comedy scene with excellence.

LEVEL IV: INTERMEDIATE COMEDY EXERCISES, SERIES C

THIS IS THE LAST GROUP OF EXERCISES IN THE INTERMEDIATE level, and are the most demanding in this series. You will learn how to become disciplined with several others on stage. You'll improve your ability to work with props and physical behavior. You'll also have the chance to bring subtlety into your comedy by immersing yourself into the absurdity of a situation, which will reinforce the adage "comedy comes out of the situation." You'll discover when you need and not need to be dominant in a scene. Have fun and stay loose!

GROUP 1 EXERCISE: LEARNING TO GIVE AND TAKE IN GROUP SCENES

There is something in acting called the "Center of Interest." An audience can only watch one action at a time. If action is taking place on stage left, the actor on stage right must remain still. This means both actors must work as a team and be aware of not hogging the scene or diffusing the center of interest. This makes it much easier for an audience to follow what's going on. Stay attuned to each other and listen, listen, listen. Be respectful of your fellow actors. If you find yourself in a scene where there's chaos, step in the middle of it and do something to grab control, even if it means yelling "Quiet!" or pretending your contact lens just fell out. Just be sure that you and your fellow actors are not trying to solve the chaos at the same time. Remember, it's not the quantity of talking; it's the quality of listening that matters. The exercise in this group will help you practice listening to each other.

TALK SOUP

This is a good exercise to help you practice giving and taking, because there are several people onstage. This improv can turn into a free-for-all, so you have to learn when to take your turn and when to allow others to speak. The offstage interviewer has to keep control of the conversation and not let it get chaotic, and the onstage actors, too, must not let get it out of control.

Everyone participating must allow the story to unfold. The offstage interviewer has to learn how to set up a scene for the other actors. His or her objective is not to be the funny one, but to help the other actors have opportunities to be funny by setting up straight lines for them.

This exercise is similar to You Are There in Chapter 5 on page 106, but it requires using your imagination even more, because you need to create the identity of the characters. While You Are There gave guidelines to follow, due to the character identity you were assigned, this exercise gives you much less information.

PEOPLE NEEDED: 5

DIRECTIONS: The offstage interviewer determines who the four actors onstage will portray, and then interviews them. The actors make up the characterizations based on the theme they are given. Some suggested themes:

Two gay couples trying to adopt a child

Four husbands who act like bachelors

Two women obsessed with two prisoners

Two boyfriends with a lot of complaints about their girlfriends, or vice versa

Four women with too much pressure in their lives

Two couples discussing whether their relationship can be saved

Two men only attracted to chubby women (with two women onstage), or vice versa

Two men only turned on by Jewish women (with two women onstage), or vice versa

Two parent-child pairs in which the kids don't get along with their parents

Four UPS or FedEx guys who like to cross dress

Two couples (not romantic) discussing how one changed the other's life

GROUP 2 EXERCISES: LEARNING HOW TO USE AND BE AFFECTED BY PROPS

Actors work with props all the time, and working with them can give you a lot back. When all your senses are alive, you're much more interesting to watch. Since props will affect your speech pattern, it is very important that you learn how to talk and use props at the same time, while making it all look natural. These exercises will help you.

THE GIN GAME

This exercise will integrate physical activity into your conversation while allowing it to affect you.

PEOPLE NEEDED: 2

SCENE: A card game.

DIRECTIONS: Two actors are onstage playing cards with each other. They can be friends, family members, or two people dating. While they are playing the card game, the actors must have a dialogue. The goal is for the actors to think and concentrate about the dialogue and not the card game, which is the prop. Some suggested scenes:

> A husband and wife on their anniversary
> A babysitter and child
> College roommates discussing their dating life
> A couple's first date
> Gossiping neighbors
> Cowboys
> Astronauts on the moon
> Women returning from a big department store sale
> Coworkers during a lunch break

FOOD SCENE

As an actor, you always want to stay open to being influenced by physical behavior. You want all of your five senses alive and kicking. This exercise provides an opportunity for the actors to eat real food and use it to create behavior tailored to the characters and the scene.

PEOPLE NEEDED: 2 or more

SCENE: Dining.

DIRECTIONS: Two actors each bring in a real dish of food. When several actors play out the scene, they can create a buffet party. Maybe there is a host or hostess who has invited one or more friends over to dine. Or maybe it's a potluck. When there are more than three actors, it is important for them to listen intently to each other so that they are not talking over each other. Use the food as a prop to enhance the dialogue. Some suggested scenes:

> A romantic meal a guy cooked for his date
> An awkward holiday dinner with a spouse and ex
> An interfaith couple invites the rabbi or priest over to dinner
> An African American woman invites a Caucasian man over for soul
>   food
> A British household in which the dining habits are extremely proper
> A date between a southern redneck and his/her girlfriend/boyfriend
> A couple's dinner date with his/her mother

A nosy neighbor comes over for dinner
A psychic comes to the dinner party
A fiancé discovers his fiancée is terrible in the kitchen

HIRING A TEMPORARY WORKER

This is an opportunity to explore physical comedy and to how to use props, even when they are not there.

PEOPLE NEEDED: 2

DIRECTIONS: An employer has to hire someone to do the work for an absentee employee. A temporary assistant enters with no idea of what the job is going to be. The humor comes out of the assistant finding the job extremely challenging, which eventually leads to disaster. Some suggested scenarios:

A temporary celebrity assistant who is star struck
A temporary medical assistant who becomes nauseous from just putting on a mask
A temporary baker who continually samples all the cakes
A temporary gardener who is allergic to flowers
A temporary dental assistant who continually sneezes
A temporary busboy who is very clumsy and drops the dishes
A temporary typist with extremely long nails who can't touch the keys
A temporary transcriber who can't remember anything
A temporary dyslexic file clerk who misfiles
A temporary receptionist who stutters

GROUP 3 EXERCISE: USING INNUENDOES IN A CREDIBLE WAY

Sex makes the world go round, but there is always a fine line one has to be careful not to cross. The British are masters at double entendre comedy involving love and sex. The restaurant scene in the movie *When Harry Met Sally* is a great example of an innuendo where the envelope is pushed, yet is still on the side of decency.

AFTER MAKING LOVE

In this exercise the actors learn to be real, subtle, and true to the scene, and allow the humor to come out of the situation.

PEOPLE NEEDED: 2

Scene: A couple in a bed.

Directions: Two people sit next to each other in chairs, while a person off-stage designates the characters and their situation. The background of the scene is that they met previously in a normal, everyday situation, one thing led to another, and they ended up making love.

The improv starts when both actors begin to recognize each other from the past sexual encounter. Focus on subtlety; do not overplay the scene. Rather, allow the comedy to come out of this bizarre situation. Stay silent at the very start, and please don't rush the dialogue at the beginning. Some suggested relationships are:

A fashion designer and model after a runway show
A psychic and client
An usher and patron in a theater after the movie
Two janitors cleaning an office building during their nightshift
A pool boy and rich housewife
An Avon lady and a customer
A theatrical agent and actress
A Chippendale dancer and audience groupie
An exterminator and housewife
A waitress and customer after closing

GROUP 4 EXERCISE: LEARNING TO BE ONSTAGE BY YOURSELF

It can be challenging to be onstage by yourself and feel completely confident, since all eyes are on you. Here are some specific rules on how to be effective onstage by yourself:

Take it moment by moment and learn not to rush.
Allow the audience to follow what's happening.
Show various colors and facets of your personality through a broad
　　range in your acting and transitions.
When you are look over the audience area, use the complete
　　spectrum of the theater, playing to an imaginary balcony.
Learn that a simple turn of the head or a small gesture can be very
　　telling to an audience.
Love owning the stage. There are great feelings to have in this
　　situation, so be committed and involved in what you are doing.
Build a momentum toward your finale. Take all your feelings and
　　build them.

BEING A STAR ON AN EMPTY STAGE

This one-person exercise will allow you to take ownership of the stage even further, because you cannot depend on anyone else. It also gives you an opportunity to mentally picture the imaginary person you will be talking to. For comedy actors, seeing is everything. You must really see the details of the imaginary person in order to bring him or her to life. Believability is vital. This exercise is fun to do several times, and try different things. It's a long scene, with several phases.

PEOPLE NEEDED: 1

DIRECTIONS: You've gone backstage to meet the star of a musical, rock concert, Broadway play, ballet, TV show, circus, opera, stand-up, or mime performance.

Begin stage right and pretend you are talking to the star backstage. Play out to the audience. Visualize a specific celebrity, and have a thirty-second conversation with the star, saying his or her full name out loud so that the audience will know whom you're talking about. Congratulate the star on the performance.

Next, cross to stage left, as if you think the exit is located there. When you get there, you realize that this isn't the exit, so you turn around and slowly go back to stage right, still seeking the exit.

As you start to walk back, you suddenly realize that you are alone at the back of the stage, where you just saw the performance. You look around to see if anyone is there, and then begin walking forward, awestruck by the stage, the balcony, etc. This is everyone's fantasy, to be on a major stage all alone, where you can do anything you want. Begin inspecting the stage area, using your sense memory. Look out front and imagine this magnificent theater right in front of you. You do not want to rush this at all; take the moments to make the situation real, as if you were really in a theater alone. Also mix in feelings of concern, such as whether you might get caught.

All of a sudden, you recognize that since you are alone, you can perform center stage, doing something in the same genre as the show you just saw. For instance, if the star you met was Rod Stewart, start singing a rock song. If he or she was a stand-up comedian like, say, Jerry Seinfeld, perform a stand-up routine. Do this part for about a minute and a half to two minutes.

Just as you're starting to get lost in your performance, pretend you hear someone coming. Start to panic and then make a quick exit to upstage right. Just as you get to that corner, take one glance back out front and show the audience how passionate you are about performing one day on that stage. Then exit. You may very well end up with a great monologue for yourself.

GROUP 5 EXERCISES: LEARNING TO BE THE DOMINANT ACTOR IN THE SCENE

In some scenes you may play a lesser role. But when you are the dominant actor in the scene, you have to take command. The scene depends on how you move the energy. Your objective is to keep propelling the scene forward. You cannot wait for someone else to lead it. If you are really working the scene with everything you've got, you should be exhausted by the end.

RESTAURANTS AROUND THE WORLD

The dominant actor must really stretch and be a character that can do it all in this exercise. The other two actors will practice being the straight men for the dominant actor.

PEOPLE NEEDED: 3

SCENE: A restaurant that is short-staffed.

DIRECTIONS: The actor onstage is the owner or manager of a restaurant that can be located anywhere in the world. The dominant actor must use the appropriate accent or dialect of the restaurant's location. The other two actors are American tourists on vacation, and it's their first night out in the town where the restaurant is located. Remember, the two actors must play the straight men for the dominant actor. For whatever reason (it's a cheesy place, the wait staff did not come in, or any reason you want to make up) the dominant actor must perform the responsibilities of the maitre d', the waiter, and the entertainment (but not the cook—assume the cook is there). The comedy comes from the dominant actor, who must wear three hats to keep the customers happy. Some suggestions of where to situate the scene (choose either a country or type of restaurant) are:

Countries:
Africa
Alabama
Australia
Britain
China
Cuba
France

India
Ireland
Israel
Italy
Japan
Mexico
Norway
Russia
Scotland
Sweden

Types of Restaurants:
All-you-can-eat buffet
Beverly Hills celebrity hangout
Cafeteria
Deli
Macrobiotic
Seafood
Soul food
Southern

PEOPLE'S COURT

This exercise allows one actor to learn how to take the reins and lead the comedy stage. It also helps teach the *Seinfeld* model of making a big deal out of nothing.

PEOPLE NEEDED: 3

DIRECTIONS: When a case is too big for the Superior Court or small claims court, the last resort is our very own People's Court. Two chairs are placed at a distance from each other onstage. The offstage person who plays the judge is seated in the audience area at a reasonable distance away from the actors. The two actors onstage stand next to their chairs. The judge says, "Court is now in session. May I hear your problem please?"

One actor plays the plaintiff and states his or her name and complaint. The judge gives the defendant a chance to identify whom they are and state his or her defense. The humor ensues as the judge keeps going back and forth, stirring the pot and embellishing the conflict to move it along. Some suggestions of possible complaints are:

A client who had long hair and just wanted a trim, but the
hairdresser cut it all off

A lady who brought her dog in for grooming and discovered the
groomer dyed the dog's hair without permission

A neighbor who had hosed down his or her next-door neighbor in
retaliation for a late night party

A mechanic who advertised a $29.95 lube job and ruined the
customer's car engine

A travel agent who booked a client on what turned out to be a
nightmare vacation

A weatherperson who made an erroneous weather report and is
being sued by a TV viewer, who organized his or her vacation plans
according to the weatherperson's report.

A bride who ordered a bridle gown and wound up with a bridle
miniskirt

A mother who accuses her son of trying to disown her

GROUP 6 EXERCISES: STRETCHING THE COMEDY IMAGINATION

Stretching your comedy imagination is how you grow as a comedy actor.
You have to open yourself up, get outside your comfort zone. The exercises in this group will teach you to think more creatively. You're in a comedy
playground to play, take chances, fall on your tush and look silly. Bring out
your inner child and stretch your naturally vivid imagination.

THE LETTER

As you let this scenario unfold, you and your partner will learn how to be
in tune and connected.

PEOPLE NEEDED: 2

DIRECTIONS: Two people are seated onstage with some distance between
them. One of the rules of the exercise is that the two face the audience,
never looking at each other. Actor #1 starts reading out loud a letter that
he or she received from Actor #2. Simultaneously, Actor #2 is writing on a
piece of paper in the same attitude that Actor #1 is reading.

After Actor #1 reads the letter to Actor #2, they switch. Actor #2 then
reads the letter that Actor#1 has written back after he or she read the initial letter. Meanwhile Actor #1 is writing as if he or she is creating the
response letter. Some examples of unique relationships:

Prisoner and a prison groupie from the outside
Rock star and fan club member
Husband who went out to take the trash and stayed away for ten years
Russian ballet dancer that came to America and is corresponding
    with her/his former partner in Russia
Teacher writing to their former student
Woman writing to her psychologist, letting him know she has a crush
    on him
Agent writing to his/her client, letting him or her go
Neighbor writing to another neighbor about what he or she really
    thinks about him or her

INANIMATE OBJECTS

This is a great exercise to allow yourself to go for the silly and embrace physical comedy. The two actors have an opportunity to give life to inanimate objects.

PEOPLE NEEDED: 2

DIRECTIONS: Two actors get into physical positions to depict the inanimate objects below. They emulate the objects and act out their physicality to the best of their ability. The actors can respond to imaginary people that might interact with them. For instance, the actor playing an evening gown in the closet might imagine a woman opening the closet to see what she's going to wear for a dressy affair. If she chooses the gown you're portraying, you would physically act out how she might treat you and verbalize how you would feel and what you observe. Some suggestions for inanimate objects:

Hot and cold water faucets in the sink
Apples on an apple tree
An evening gown and a tuxedo in a closet
Brake and gas pedal
Salt and pepper shakers

ANIMAL EXERCISE

The exercise requires two actors. To the best of their abilities, the actors get into physical positions that best exemplify the animals they're portraying. They talk to each other as if they were those specific animals. The humor lies in bringing the animals to life and talking about the things they would talk about. For example, one cow might say to the other, "Is that all you can say, *Moo*?" or "I'm your mother. Talk to me." Some suggested animals:

Cats at home by themselves
Chipmunks in the woods
Cows in a field
Dogs in a store window
Fleas on a dog
Hens in a hen house
Mice in a maze
Monkeys in a zoo
Ostriches
Snakes in Australia
Swans in a lake
Turtles in a tank
Walruses in the Arctic

PUBLICITY

The purpose of this exercise is for one actor to have fun playing a larger than life public relations person who's job is to convince the other actor that he or she desperately needs publicity.

PEOPLE NEEDED: 2

DIRECTIONS: The scene opens with the first actor already onstage playing the over-the-top public relations expert, while the second actor enters portraying the person determining whether or not this PR wiz can help his or her career. The first actor gets to exaggerate and embellish, so that the dullest job in the world sounds newsworthy. The second actor is completely honest in telling the PR actor the truth of his or her own particular life.

This is a great exercise for stretching the comedy imagination and being able to think on your feet very quickly. Taking true facts about the other actor's life and career and giving them a twist will result in getting the second actor excited on how fabulous his or her life and career really are. For example, you might have the second actor pretend to have a mundane job, such as an exterminator, carpet cleaner, wart remover, crossing guard, etc. The PR person will have a field day acting up a storm and creating great scenarios on how he or she can sell the mundane job to the media.

ACTORS CHOOSE THE PREMISE

This is a scene in which the actors pick a location below or come up with their own. They must confer with each other to conceive their own premise. It's important for the actors to also develop their improvisational/writing skills, so they can stretch their imagination in creating story structure.

PEOPLE NEEDED: 2 to 4

DIRECTIONS: The actors get five minutes to converse offstage before they do their scene.

Suggested Locations:
Baseball stadium
Botox party
Cocktail party
Dentist office
Gym
Hair salon
Hospital
Hotel
Library
Military recruiting office
Office
Pet spa
Restaurant

LEVEL V: ADVANCED COMEDY EXERCISES

NOW THAT YOU'VE COMPLETED THE PREVIOUS TRAINING, YOU are now ready to move into the comedy Olympics. You've done really well if you've gotten to this point, and should congratulate yourself and feel a strong sense of accomplishment. So it's time to go for the gold!

We need to do some heavy lifting and utilize what we've gone through in life to our advantage. Tapping into our emotional recall is necessary to bring our true self into the work. So don't resist this important element. The exercises in Group 2 are a training ground for learning to impersonate those around you. Jamie Foxx is a master at this, and can deliver an immediate funny quip on those he works with or those in the news, because he always gives himself the freedom to play and be silly. Put that ingredient in your own comedy recipe.

The exercises in Group 3 are all about creating a comedy twist or spin, which is very important in the world of sitcoms, as producers are looking for that extra creativity. The Group 4 exercises are about stretching yourself to the max, and you will be amazed at what brilliance may come out of your comedy imagination, so get out that camcorder and watch what you've come up with so you can fine tune it at a later date. Go into the Group 5 exercises and throw caution to the wind. I believe that singing is the final step to complete comedy freedom and can bring a tremendous amount of joy to your creative world. Enjoy!

GROUP 1 EXERCISES: EMOTIONAL MEMORY

Here's a chance to connect the dots in your life. The Lifelong Picture exercise has helped so many of my students discover aspects of their lives that they hadn't thought about for awhile, which can be true for you as well. This is really fun to do in a small group, so that you can each be a support for each other. By physicalizing the traits of another person you learn to expand your comedy toolbox. The smart thing to do is after you do the scene, keep playing with those traits, and see where it takes you. The Big Chill exercise taps into your ability to move into the future, while satirizing your past with those you are working with.

LIFE LONG PICTURE EXERCISE

Gather photos from your life, from birth to your present age. Find fifteen to twenty-five photos and put them in chronological order. This is a "connect the dots in your life" exercise. I created this premise after I saw Meryl Streep in the final scene of the movie *The Bridges of Madison County*.

Meryl had to get very emotional at the end of the film, as she read the letter from Clint Eastwood's character. When you read a moving letter like that, one might ask how you bring all the right emotions to it. If the scene needs to be humorous, what picture might provoke your funny bone? Here is an option to prepare yourself for such a scene.

PEOPLE NEEDED: 2 or more

DIRECTIONS: Lay out all the photos and pick them up one by one. Pick up the first picture, from when you were the youngest. Allow yourself to be filled with emotion. Feel that emotion, and when you're ready, share that feeling with the people in your group, as well as a concise description of the circumstances of the picture. (If necessary, this exercise could be done with you and one other person.) Someone in the audience then writes, on the back of the photo, the emotion you talked about, so it will be documented for you. Then in the future, if you need to feel sad or humorous, you can look at the photo before doing a scene. It's a preparatory tool you can use at anytime.

After you've gone through all the pictures and completed the entire process, the audience members figure out what three qualities are your most consistent, from birth to now. Then at the count of three, the audience says them together to you. An example might be, "Solid, giving, and fun-loving." This allows you to walk away with a sense of what three qualities ties your life together.

The last part of the exercise is to think of a song that is an oldie-but-goodie for you, that hits your emotional hot button whenever you hear it. Then think of the person who comes up in your mind whenever you listen to that song. Sing about thirty to forty seconds of the song to the audience; it's another way to prepare for a scene before you go onstage.

By linking your life together, synthesizing in three words your most consistent qualities, and associating a song with your emotions, you can add emotional facility to your comedy-acting arsenal.

REMINISCING EXERCISE

Two actors are seated onstage. Both chairs are facing the audience, angled so that the actors cannot look at each other. One actor reminisces for a few sentences about anything in his or her life. When the first actor stops talking, the other actor starts by using a word from those sentences and taking it in a different direction. They continue reminiscing about real events from their lives or made up events.

For example, Actor #1 may talk for a few sentences, and include a mention of chocolate mousse cake. When Actor #1 is finished talking, Actor #2 picks up on the word "mousse" and reminisces about a moose he or she saw in Vermont when hiking. Thus, Actor #2 takes the word and moves it in a different direction.

Then when Actor #2 has spoken for a few sentences, Actor #1 might pick up on "hiking" and talk about a hitchhiking trip he or she took. Remember, the purpose of the reminiscing is to see vivid pictures in your mind and make them real to the audience.

The benefit of this exercise is to give the actors an opportunity to see real pictures in their minds. When the actor sees the picture, the audience does as well.

BIG CHILL REUNION

This exercise is based on the film *The Big Chill,* in which friends from college reunite after a few years. It's a chance for the participants to use real information they have about each other, or make up storylines about what could have possibly happened in their lives.

PEOPLE NEEDED: 2 or more

DIRECTIONS: A small group of actors are onstage together meeting ten, twenty, or thirty years in the future (just choose a year). They reminisce about what their lives have been like since they've seen each other. Using their imaginations, they talk about what has happened in their lives, as they think backwards from the present day. Keep it real and subtle, and allow it to fully encapsulate the personality of each participant.

GROUP 2 EXERCISES: PHYSICALIZING SOMEONE ELSE'S PERSONA

These exercises will help you hone the art of picking up on someone else's physical traits and making them yours. This allows you to step out of your own persona and move into someone else's.

AFTER CLASS SECRETS

This premise is designed for you to use everything you've noticed about someone else's life and persona, steal from him or her, and make it your own. It's best for a group of people who've been working together for a while and know each others' specific traits and qualities.

PEOPLE NEEDED: 2

DIRECTIONS: One actor is onstage as the other enters. Pretend it's just after an acting class. Actor #1 stops Actor #2 to compliment him or her on a "quality" he or she possesses, and asks Actor #2 to please explain how to embody that quality. Actor #2 does whatever is necessary to teach Actor #1 how to be like him or her. If you're Actor #2, don't just tell Actor #1 how to do it—physically act out all the mannerisms and body postures of your particular quality, using the entire stage.

Actor #1 genuinely wants to develop the behavior, accent, and "quality" of Actor #2.

For instance, if one actor is somewhat on the nerdy side, he or she may be sent in to learn from the big jock. He might say, "Oh hi, Rocky. Some of my friends have said I need to become more of a manly man, so I was wondering if you could show me how to act more like you. You've got that jock thing going on, and I think you can help me." The person onstage has to then teach the nerd how to be more like a jock through breaking down the way he or she walks, talks, gestures, and behaves.

In another example, a straight-laced librarian type could learn from the sexy bimbo type how to be more effective and flirtatious with men. Or if one gal is on the heavyset side, she may come onstage to work with a gal who is a model type. The model would teach the other how to walk, suck in the cheeks, and have that glazed, seductive, runway look.

It's all about one learning from another's physicality, accent, or dialect. The comedy comes in as one person tries to get the other to be exactly like him or her.

BECOME EACH OTHER

At the end of your working session, it's a lot of fun to do this exercise. Come up with any improv you want to perform. The premise of the scene you come up with is not important, as the key element is playing each other, utilizing all of your observations of them.

PEOPLE NEEDED: At least 4

DIRECTIONS: The acting group is split in half and positioned on either side of the stage. Each actor is assigned a partner from the other side that he or she will portray as a character in a two- or three-person scene. Here's an example of how this falls together:

John, Phil, and Mary are on one side of the stage and Greg, Joe, and Sally are on the other. John will impersonate Greg, and Greg will impersonate John. Phil will impersonate Joe, and Joe will impersonate Phil. Mary will impersonate Sally, and Sally will impersonate Mary.

John, Phil, and Mary will be in a scene together, discussing what they are going to do for an improv, which really is only an excuse for these three actors to impersonate the other three actors. You want to make sure you call each other by the names of the people you're portraying. You can change clothes or do anything you can to be that other person. The point of this exercise is to use your powers of observation and completely impersonate someone else.

GROUP 3 EXERCISES: CREATING A COMEDY TWIST OR SPIN

It's vital to nurture your ability to spin something and make it funny. You and everyone you work with are responsible for twisting and bending the circumstances to bring out the humor.

FAMOUS SCENES FROM FAMOUS MOTION PICTURES

Use some of these famous scenes to create humor.

PEOPLE NEEDED: 3

DIRECTIONS: A cable network (such as E! Television Network) wants non-actors and new actors to play famous scenes from famous movies. One person is the casting director, and the other two actors—either playing themselves or characters—are auditioning for the parts. The casting director interviews them for a minute or so and finds out if they have any show biz experience. Then he or she informs the actors what scene they are to depict from which movie.

The casting director then becomes the director of the scene, stopping and starting it, constantly correcting the actors when necessary in a similar way to the Commercial Interruptus exercise on page 60. The casting director plays the straight man, while the actors play the scene for humor, using literary license to change the movie to make it funny. You can exaggerate, overplay, be absurd, change the most famous line, etc.—anything to give it a comedic twist. Even if you haven't seen the movie, you can still play the parts using the descriptions provided. (Or choose a movie you have seen outside of the suggested list below.) Some possible movie scenes:

The scene is from *Body Heat,* and takes place in the south: very hot and sweaty. William Hurt is trying to knock down the door of the house inhabited by the sexy Kathleen Turner. It's a push-pull type of scene, where she wants him to come in because she's turned on, but she's afraid to. He's banging on the door, asking her to open it and she's running back and forth, yelling at him in one moment to go away, and the next moment telling him, "Oh, I don't know what to do, I'm so confused."

The final scene from *The Crying Game*, when one character finds out the girl he is dating is not really a woman, but a man. They've been out to dinner and are talking quietly back at the apartment. The one who has the gender issue tells the other character, "I'm just going to freshen up," and then comes back out in something that is a little revealing. This scene is to be completely mimed and acted in good taste. It's all about the innuendo.

The Tom Cruise/Jack Nicholson scene in *A Few Good Men*, in which Tom is a military lawyer interrogating Jack Nicholson—playing a military commander—about why he ordered the Code Red. Tom keeps bombarding Jack with questions, finally saying, "Commander, I need to know the truth," and Jack replies with the famous line, "You can't handle the truth." The humor should come in the build-up of what leads into the final line.

Susan Sarandon as a serious, pious nun and Sean Penn as the condemned man in *Dead Man Walking*. It's the last conversation they have before he is executed, and she asks what she can get him before he dies. He may order a very detailed meal for his last dinner but keep changing the order.

The scene from *Chinatown* when Jack Nicholson's character confronts Faye Dunaway's character, and she reveals her daughter is also her sister. In this scene, the actress could get confused and say that her mother is her sister, or is my sister my mother, or is my mother my mother?

A scene from *A Beautiful Mind* in which the wife confronts her husband to tell him she thinks he's nuts, because he keeps telling her there are spies all over the place. He denies it adamantly, saying he's a mathematical genius.

The scene in *Capote* in which famous author Truman Capote visits the accused killer of a family in Kansas while researching a book about the crime; Capote is gay and looks as though he might be attracted to the prisoner.

The scene from Hitchcock's *The Birds* in which Tippi Hedren's character reacts to all the birds attacking her when she enters the house. You need to pretend that the birds are attacking you—so don't hold back. The casting director can have a field day directing the actor playing the Hedren role.

CASTING CALL

This is an exercise to help you become more versatile in developing sketch characters more quickly. Imagine you are up for a part in a movie called "Show Business High," about a fictional high school in Hollywood, California. There is a casting session for the film, and below is the list of roles that are available. You will be auditioning for one of these roles. Figure out who would you like to audition for and give birth to that character. You can either have an interviewer ask you questions, or you can come out in character and just talk about yourself.

One actor does this at a time. Then you can create scenes out of the people who were auditioning, as another improvisation to follow.

Jean Paul Francoise: Mime Coach
Speaks French existentialism. Studied the writings of Jean Paul Sartre. Continually raves about the heroics of Joan of Arc and thinks everything's better in Paris.

Sally Titowsky: Dietician
Russian exchange student who became head dietician. Everything in her kitchen is immaculate, and she is very enthusiastic about the nutritional value of the food she prepares.

Moose Skowrom: Gym teacher and personal fitness trainer
Thinks he's the gift to the world. Constantly flexing and showing off his muscles to anyone and everyone.

Joanna Pakula: Polish actress and exchange student
Just arrived from Poland on a freighter. Is in love with Leonardo DiCaprio and desperately wants to meet him.

Millie Fortensky: Tap dance teacher
Tap is her life; she loves teaching tap morning, noon, and night. She is bubbly, outgoing, and effervescent, a former Rockette in New York.

Cora Rudolsky: Dean of the school
Is controlled by old show biz standards. Loves to perform herself and cries easily when she sees someone else perform well. Can be tough when necessary and her hobby is astrology.

Milton Perlman: Janitor
Older man who was big in the golden years of Hollywood. He loves being connected to the business and enjoys talking about the good old days.

Marilyn Miller: Student
She's an actress wannabe from a trailer park in the south. Is completely obsessed with Marilyn Monroe and knows everything about her.

Bubba Packwood: Student
Looks like Jethro from *The Beverly Hillbillies,* and is hoping the school will do a production of it so he can play the part.

Lisa and Liza: Twin students
They love jocks, the bigger the better. Constantly squeal and titter like giggly girls as they constantly make up school cheers. They are never apart.

Ira Franklin: School sales counselor
Ultimate high-powered manic salesperson, whose job is to bring students into the school at any cost; otherwise he might lose his job.

Penny Blumberg: Spoiled Beverly Hills girl
A Jewish American princess type. President of the Hebrew club—and Vice President as well.

Veronica Lane: Beauty pageant winner
Goes with Billy Bob. All she cares about is winning a beauty pageant.

Willie Wayans: A cousin of the Wayans brothers
He's the only member of the Wayans family that doesn't have talent, and the family just pawned him off to the school to see if they can do anything with him.

Janine Hart: Singing teacher
Former *American Idol* contestant. Loves to talk about her time on the show and how close she got to making it. (She didn't even make the top 100.)

Consuela Lopez: Actress
Wants to be the next J-Lo, and never stops shaking her bootie and doing her Beyonce bounce.

Ina B. Miller: Journalist
She writes for the local paper and knows all the gossip on everyone. Her father Milton Miller is on the board.

Billy Bo Bob: Texan
Constantly smiles. He dreams of having his own worm farm. Some people in the school think he's going to be the next Brad Pitt.

Vito Stunad: Maintenance
Builds the sets for the high school productions. A "deez," "dem," and "doze" kind of guy from the Bronx.

Suzanne Hunt: Beverly Hills matron and sponsor
Has all the material things in life, but has a boring marriage. Likes to flirt with the guys in a subtle way.

Marty Fox: Agent
Hollywood agent. Always on the prowl on campus for pretty girls.

Bud Feldman: Stand-up comedy teacher
Loves to do one-liners and doesn't care if anyone else laughs because he laughs at his own jokes.

GROUP 4 EXERCISES: VERSATILITY

It's time to put it all together and show your range. The following exercises will sharpen your capability to display the many facets of your talent.

IMPROV GROUPS AUDITIONING

This is an exercise to do once you've been working with the other actors for a while. Three or more actors are onstage auditioning as an acting repertory group. For example, you might introduce yourself to the audience the following way. "We are the Huckabees, and do a variety of improvisation. Our other styles of acting include Tennessee Williams, Shakespeare, and everything in between." As a group you create a framework to show off your versatility, as you're making it up in the moment. The scenario is to sell your group to people who might hire you. It's fast paced with quick transitions. Get together with the other actors to decide what you're going to do, and then go full blast. Give the group a name, and have fun showing off your versatility in all that you've been learning so far.

TV SPECIAL ON A CELEBRITY

This is a group exercise, where as a group you get to show your complete versatility. The context in this example is that you all are involved in the life of Michael Jackson. (You can follow up with any other celebrity's life if you like.)

Before doing the scene, you all sit down and write down what people might be involved in the celebrity's life. Then give the list to the interviewer. Don't write down any notes about what you are going to say, just who you are. Here's an example if we were doing a show on Michael Jackson.

The actors onstage will portray people who have been involved in Michael's life, and are asked questions by an off-stage interviewer sitting in the audience. Below are some choices:

Michael's lawyers
His clothing stylist and make-up artist
His new image consultants
President and vice-president of Michael's fan club
Doctors treating his alleged disease
His plastic surgeons
A reporter who has interviewed him
Someone who knows him in Bahrain where he lives now
Oprah Winfrey and Dr. Phil
His former wives: Lisa Marie Presley and Debbie Rowe
His two children
His new managers

THE PEOPLE IN THE LIFE OF YOUR COMEDY SKETCH CHARACTER

Use the same concept as above, but apply it to the life of one of your comedy sketch characters. For example, one of my students came up with a character named Teddy Israel, a woman who lives alone in New York and who used to be an old show biz veteran. We used this exercise to come up with all the people in Teddy's life. You can take any character you are working on to create other people in their life, which deepens the history and background of your character. In Teddy's case, we came up with:

Her agent
Estranged daughter
Hairdresser
Last boyfriend
Dress shop where she gets big discounts
Next-door neighbor
Card-playing friend
Veteran character actor who worked with her in the "Caravan of
    Stars"
Counselor
Former lesbian lover

"FULLY COMMITTED"

In this exercise inspired by the play *Fully Committed*, by Becky Mode, one person is onstage using a telephone with multiple phone lines. The character works as a reservation taker at any kind of restaurant, where customers call in continuously in the daytime for dinner reservations at night. An offstage person yells out who is on what line. For instance:

Line #1 is a demanding French woman
Line #2 is a celebrity
Line #3 is your mother
Line #4 is the restaurant owner
Line #5 is a bratty child

The actor onstage answers the phone as the reservation taker, saying, "Hi, this is [name of restaurant]." Then the same actor plays the person calling in, based on what the offstage person has assigned him. The actor must juggle multiple phone calls, playing multiple characters, while the offstage person intermittently calls out the line that needs answering by saying, "Ring, ring, back to line #4," reminding the actor onstage of the character. This is an outstanding opportunity to be completely uncensored and do your own mini one-person show.

LIP SYNC

This is a solo exercise that needs to be prepped and rehearsed in advance.

PEOPLE NEEDED: 1

DIRECTIONS: Find a scene from a film or TV show. Get it on to an audio-cassette or a CD for playback. You can find a clip from different genres such as suspense, horror, comedy, soap opera, musical, or one of your own choosing. If you want, you can mix old and new films. You then lip sync to the tape and act it out. Two to three minutes is plenty of time to work with, and you will definitely have to memorize the lines. You don't have to play all the characters in the scene, you can simply select the one you like the best. Then when you are ready to display your performance, do it in front of your group.

VENTRILOQUIST

This is a perfect exercise to explore the art of ventriloquism, while allowing you to create another persona. The switching quickly back and forth from yourself to another persona will sharpen your timing.

PEOPLE NEEDED: 1

DIRECTIONS: This is an exercise that requires one person onstage. Put a sock or a puppet on your hand and play straight out to the audience. Create a different persona for the puppet, using a different voice. Then have a two to three minute conversation with the puppet. You could also use a dummy or a stuffed animal, if that is more appealing. The objective is to really believe you're talking to that other persona.

Oscar-winning actor Sir Anthony Hopkins shared with me an exercise for perfecting the craft of ventriloquism. Place a new pencil with the eraser side in your mouth and talk while the pencil is in your mouth. This allows you to get the words out without moving your mouth. Hopkins used this technique when preparing for his starring role in the film *Magic*.

INSTANT ARGUMENT

This exercise will require you to be in tune with your acting partner.

PEOPLE NEEDED: 2

DIRECTIONS: This is where you start the argument off at a "10," and must utilize razor sharp listening. One actor enters, and either participant starts exploding at the other, as if there were a time bomb ready to go off. Remember not to talk into each other. The formula to follow is that one person talks, while the other listens. The idea is not to step on each other and not to lower the energy level. You still need to derive comedy from the situation. And with two people going nuts onstage, it's vital to pay close attention and be completely in tune with each other. Some suggested relationships:

Stripper and nightclub owner
Waitress and chef
Hairstylist and client
Parent and teacher
Agent and actor
Mechanic and customer
Interior designer and housewife
Cruise director and captain
Lawyer and secretary
Doctor and patient

GROUP 5 EXERCISES: ADVANCED SONG IN COMEDY

You are now ready to stretch your comedy rubber band a little further and integrate singing into your work, which is incredibly freeing for a comedic actor.

ALL-SINGING

This exercise allows the actors to further break down their inhibitions about singing, while helping each other create a story. In this exercise, you have to do an entire improv scene in song. Remember, it's not the quality of your voice that counts, but your commitment to really go full throttle. This premise peels the onion and brings a lot of inner joy while you're doing it. Comedy is all about taking risks, and the bigger the risk, the larger the gain!

PEOPLE NEEDED: 2

DIRECTIONS: One person is onstage while the other enters. The location is designated. Don't forget, the entire exercise is done in song. Instead of the actors talking, they are singing, while simultaneously still being very true to the scene. You can use any melody you want and can change melodies throughout. During the course of the scene, work together in harmony to find certain moments to sing together. This is like creating your own musical comedy on the spot. Both actors can do different styles of music, such as country western, blues, jazz, Broadway, gospel, opera, hip hop, rap, or they can make up their own style. They can also create their own dance movements. It's a chance to be zany, crazy, and wild, while still being believable.

The actors need to get very involved physically in the situation. Some of their physical behavior will affect their singing and movements in the scene. Actors sometimes rely too much on the verbal and mental. When you get physically free, you find other ways of communicating comedically. Some suggested locations:

Barbershop
Beauty shop
Bookstore
Butcher shop
Cab
Control tower
Cop/speeder
Courtroom
Date's home
Doctor's office
Fish store
Funeral parlor
Gift shop
Lingerie shop
Meat market
Movie set
Office
On the bus
Plane
Police station
Psychiatrist's office
Racetrack
Restaurant
Shoe store
Travel agency
Unemployment line
Zoo

SONG SUBTEXT EXERCISE: THE WORLD OF MUSICAL COMEDY

Choose a song that is realistic for your singing or non-singing ability. The exercise is not really about the quality of your singing—there are many wonderful talk/patter songs available if you don't carry a tune well. Go out and learn a Broadway show song, not a pop song. Pick a song that is right for you physically, and something that will serve you if you ever have to audition for a musical. Go online and download a song, or get a CD of a recording, or borrow a song from a friend. Learn the song so you can sing it completely from memory. Also, get the sheet music and a blank new audiocassette or CD, bring it to a pianist, and ask him or her to record the song for you. If you get it recorded by someone near you, try to imitate the pace of the song from the original show recording.

When you have it memorized and have practiced with your audio accompaniment, you are ready to perform. Bring a boombox or CD player.

Step 1: You need an offstage interviewer to ask you some questions about your life. You are just being yourself. The goal of the interviewer is to lead you into expressing some emotional hot button within you. He or she will have to probe until something lights you up. It may make you angry, sad, joyous, or upset. Then the interviewer asks you who the person is in your life that is connected to that emotion.

Step 2: Improvise a conversation with the person connected to the emotion that has lit you up. Talk to that imagined person for a short time, as the offstage interviewer listens. When the interviewer feels you are emotionally ready, he or she will turn on the boombox or CD player to start the accompaniment.

Step 3: Don't change a thing once you start to sing the song. Take the exact same emotion with you as you sing the song. You are emotionally ready, singing to the person you chose in step 2, feeling completely connected inside. This is the prime focus of the exercise: To feel connected inside and to be extremely specific in seeing the person to whom you are communicating your message.

SOME SUGGESTED SONGS:

For men with limited voices:
Talk Patter songs are great if you have a limited voice
"Tonight at Eight" from *She Loves Me*
"Willkommen" from *Cabaret*
"To Be a Performer" from *Little Me*
"Mr. Cellophane" from *Chicago*
"Miracle of Miracles" from *Fiddler on the Roof*

"Comedy Tonight" from *A Funny Thing Happened on the Way to the Forum*
"Officer Krupke" from *West Side Story*
"Mama a Rainbow" from *Minnie's Boys*
"Get Me to the Church on Time" from *My Fair Lady*

For men with good voices:
"Try to Remember" from *The Fantastiks*
"Soon It's Going to Rain" from *The Fantastiks*
"Day by Day" from *Godspell*
"Anyone Can Whistle" from *Anyone Can Whistle*
"Sunrise Sunset" from *Fiddler on the Roof*
"Where is Love" from *Oliver*
"She Loves Me" from *She Loves Me*
"A Lot of Living to Do" from *Bye Bye Birdie*
"Old Devil Moon" from *Finian's Rainbow*
"Maria" from *West Side Story*
"On a Clear Day" from *On a Clear Day You Can See Forever*

For women with limited voices:
"I'm Sandra Dee" from *Grease*
"Maybe This Time" from *Cabaret*
"Sweet Charity" from *Sweet Charity*
"Big Spender" from *Sweet Charity*
"Hey Look Me Over" from *Wildcat*
"All That Jazz" from *Chicago*
"Cabaret" from *Cabaret*

For women with good voices:
"Where Am I Going?" from *Sweet Charity*
"Putting it Together" from *Sunday in the Park with George*
"Whatever Lola Wants" from *Damn Yankees*
"The Millers' Son" from *A Little Night Music*
"Send in the Clowns" from *A Little Night Music*
"And I Am Telling You, I'm Not Going" from *Dreamgirls*
"Summertime" from *Porgy and Bess*

COMEDY
LEGENDS

IN MY CAREER I HAVE HAD THE GREAT FORTUNE TO INTERVIEW, work with, or teach some wonderfully talented comedy legends. It is my pleasure to be able to pass on some tips that I learned from them to help you in your comedy journey. It is very important to learn from those who came before you, as I believe the only way to figure out where you're going is to learn from those who came before you. That's why I want to share my insights about those who paved the way in comedy. One of the common denominators that all of them share is their work ethic. They followed their bliss with due diligence and hard work. Each one of these stars experienced the work included in the comedy exercises you just studied.

John Larroquette

John Larroquette is a perfect example of a superb dramatic actor who was able to bring his dramatic expertise to comedic acting, and win an Emmy for it. Although he already possessed the elements of story structure and the depth of character development, he needed to become free in order to move into comedy acting. His vibe seemed heavy when I first met him.

When John was in my comedy acting class, I stretched his comedy imagination and lightened him up, which allowed him to create a very vivid comedy imagination. We worked on some of the same material that I present in this book—improvisation, written comedy scenes, and sketch comedy work. John has an amazing command of his resonant voice, which greatly contributed to his comedy. It had not been common in television to have such a resonant Shakespearean voice. In addition, John is a tall guy, and he uses every aspect of himself, completely owning who he is and using his physicality as an advantage. John realized by doing various physical comedy exercises, especially the animate and inanimate objects exercises, that he could use his size to his comedic advantage. Having a sense of what you look like and how you appear on stage or film is very beneficial to your talent, as well as to your audience. John Larroquette mastered the art of sitcom-acting through consistently doing the necessary work, and found a niche for himself playing a powerful, in-control character that can push others around him to their limits and make it funny.

Robin Williams

Robin was my classmate for two years, and I was always astounded by his creativity and imagination. When he is performing his characters, they are real to him. He has an incredible ability to impersonate everyone in show business and current events. We were in comedy class together when he landed the famous lead role of Mork in the TV sitcom *Mork and Mindy*. He had to learn to work with a script, which was a new challenge for him. The writers quickly became in tune with his strengths, and the rest is history. Robin has grown into an international star among all ages, for both drama and comedy. What I remember most about working with Robin in class was his ability to take characters from current events and add just the right spin to it to send them over the top. It is very important to know what's is going on in the world, and, more importantly, the current newsmakers. See who jumps out at you, and make sure you make use of the character bio page illustrated in Chapter 4. Trust me: it really pays to be systematic in building your characters.

I had the opportunity to interview Robin on two of my TV talk shows. He would go from character to character faster than a speeding bullet.

Robin is an only child, as am I, and creating imaginary characters to pass the time was an important part of our childhoods. Take the time to create characters in your imagination, as we talked about in Chapter 4, and experiment as much as possible. We are ourselves all the time, so think how much fun it could be to develop alternate personas.

John Ritter

John Ritter was a master at physical comedy, which is evident in the trail-blazing TV sitcom *Three's Company* co-starring Suzanne Somers and Joyce DeWitt. When we trained together in our comedy workshop for two years, he focused on pratfalls, which are falls that an actor purposely performs, making them look natural, like complete accidents. Combining the dramatic acting skills he learned when he studied under the legendary acting coach Stella Adler with his comedy training proved to be a very successful match. He exemplified what it's like to have a complete sense of freedom and abandonment as well as a great willingness to experiment, which has greatly inspired my work to this day.

I was the pledge host for the United Cerebral Palsy telethon for nine years, which was hosted by John Ritter and Henry Winkler. Our ability to be silly, yet dedicated to the cause at the same time, came from our years of experience playing off each other and working on banter in our improv training classes. Being able to banter stemmed from our listening skills, which I keep emphasizing throughout the book.

Phil Hartman

The late Phil Hartman, a *Saturday Night Live* series regular and one of the most talented celebrity impersonators of the twentieth century, always said that when you impersonate someone, you must place a picture of him or her in the space between your eyebrows, also known as your third eye, and let the picture resonate through your mind.

I was fortunate to have worked on the NBC show *Top 10*. I was the co-host with Rick Dees, and Phil was one of the series comedy stars. What was fascinating about Phil was his systematic way of working on his comedy impersonations. He believed the key was to watch videotapes of the famous people he impersonated. He would gather various TV appearances and film clips of these well-known celebrities and watch them over and over again until he completely embodied the person. I highly recommend seizing this methodology. Phil was best known for his brilliant impersonation of President Bill Clinton. When Phil impersonated Bill, he was a dead ringer for the charismatic leader. Phil also did wonderful impersonations of President Ronald Reagan and movie stars Burt Reynolds, Michael Caine, and Jack Nicholson. What made them so funny and spot on was Phil's ability to add that perfect touch that only comes from trial and error and practicing in front of audiences and fellow actors. He was always open to feedback, and it's good to stay open to those who can enhance what you are doing. But remember, you have the final word; you must always trust your own intuition.

Billy Crystal

I had the good fortune to co-host a charity benefit for cancer research with the brilliant Billy Crystal. What a memorable and wonderful situation I found myself thrown into! In his Broadway show *700 Sundays*, Billy was able to take characters from his family and bring them to life, making the audience cry and laugh in the same show. He is very much in touch with his upbringing, and has a great passion for both baseball and the entertainment industry. Billy is a man who has done it all—stand-up comedy, television, (he starred in the sitcom *Soap*), and many great movies, including *When Harry Met Sally* and *Analyze This*—not to mention his ingenious, knock-out performances whenever he hosts the Academy Awards. He creates an intimacy in a theater among the viewers and audience. When I worked with Billy, we respected each other's ability to be comedically playful, while also being professional.

What I can pass on from my time with him and observing his talent is that he uses everything in his arsenal for his comedy, such as his childhood, relatives, passion for observing people's behavior—famous or not—and an insatiable ability to push the envelope.

Jay Leno

When I interviewed Jay on my TV talk show early in his career, he talked about having performed some comedy acting and stand-up. He pursued acting, like everyone else in L.A., while he was working on his comedy routine. At the time of our interview, his goal was to be a guest on *The Tonight Show* with Johnny Carson. Little did anyone know, especially he, that he would later be the host of *The Tonight Show*.

Jay has captured that Mr. Everyman sensibility, and embodies the ability to be self-deprecating. Jay plays off his own physicality, such as his prominent chin. One unique thing about Jay is that he always finds the time to practice his monologues. His strong commitment to keeping his monologue delivery sharp is inspiring, and it pays. He also regularly plays at a comedy club called The Laugh Stop in Manhattan Beach, California, many Sundays during the year, in addition to many gigs and benefits throughout the year.

I believe his early work as an actor helps him to be a great host because he has first-hand knowledge of what his guest actors have experienced. Jay is very spontaneous, which is an absolute must when performing as a host.

Another of Jay's strengths is that he is a man of the people. He could have easily lost himself in the glitz of Beverly Hills, yet he remains real and humble, and people love it.

Jack Lemmon

Jack Lemmon is one of the legendary comedy actors of all time. Who will ever forget his brilliant performance in one on his early films, *Some Like it Hot*. It's very easy to see how Jack became a legend. When I interviewed him, Jack talked about absolutely losing himself in parts. One of my personal favorites is his performance in the film *The Prisoner of Second Avenue* with Anne Bancroft, written by his good friend, America's brilliant writer Neil Simon. Jack starred in the Neil Simon comedies *The Odd Couple*, *The Odd Couple II*, and *The Prisoner of Second Avenue*.

Jack made comedy acting look easy, yet he could turn his acting around and perform brilliant dramatic roles as well. Either way, he built a character out of what the writer gave him in the script, letting the character take him over and using his imagination to take the character to a deeper level. He would always go outside of his comfort zone. When speaking about preparing for roles, Jack confided that he immersed himself so much in the script that the crew could move him about the set in his chair and he wouldn't have a clue that he had been moved.

Phyllis Diller

Known as the first successful female stand-up, Phyllis has enjoyed success as a comedy actress. She has acted in many TV shows, as well as winning a lifetime achievement award in comedy. She started her career late in life, including stints at The Purple Onion nightclub in San Francisco. I interviewed Phyllis a few years ago, and she told me she created her comedy persona by making up an outlandish character. She chose a very short skirt and a cigarette holder as a costume and talked about her imaginary husband Fang. She played the self-deprecating housewife, and audiences worldwide related to her.

It is obvious that she had the ability to really enjoy her own material when performing. Phyllis paved the way for Joan Rivers, as well as many of the top comediennes today. Producers in TV and film loved working with her because she brought the "funny" to them.

Phyllis proves the rule that you can start your comedy career at any age. You just have to do the work and take one baby step at a time. She's enjoying her retirement from stand-up, but still writes books and is out and about socially—cracking jokes wherever she goes.

Ruth Gordon

Ruth Gordon had the ability to bring comedy to serious movies. I interviewed her twice. She was brilliant in the movie *Harold and Maude*. She brought lightness to the scary thriller *Rosemary's Baby*. This feisty actress had a lovable eccentricity about her. She is another example of how you can become even funnier with age and how you can make age work for you—and your comedy.

Henry Winkler

When I interviewed Henry Winkler, he was surprised I knew that he had been very shy as a child, but his acting journey—and the popularity of his character Fonzie on the TV sitcom *Happy Days*—took him to a greater level of confidence. Henry has a lot of spontaneity and believability, and brings both of these qualities to his work. He's an example of how an interesting person makes an interesting actor. Everything feeds the other—writing, producing, and acting. Henry serves as an inspiration: don't worry about being pigeonholed, just be creative.

Marty Feldman

The brilliant British actor Marty Feldman was a master of acting without words. He was one of the stars of the classic film *Young Frankenstein*. He successfully brought his physicality—his bulging, misaligned eyes—to his work. Having lived in England myself, I admire the Brits' ability to embrace bawdiness and bring it out in double-entendre comedy.

Marty was also a gifted comedy writer, which meant he knew story structure extremely well. He made everything look like it was improvisation. There's much to be learned by watching Marty's old movies and TV shows, as he mastered the art of farce better than most. Farce depends more on exaggeration than any of the other comedy art forms. He knew what he looked like, and used it to his advantage.

Ron Howard

Ron Howard was a child actor who brought lovability, freshness, and a midwestern wholesomeness to the TV series *The Andy Griffith Show*, which was the first spin-off in TV history, having spun off from *The Danny Thomas Show*. Ron learned from the best at an early age, working with great comedy veterans Andy Griffith and Don Knotts. Ron learned a lot about comedic timing as a child, which perhaps helped him become such a great director. On a set, he would always ask everyone involved in a TV show or film how everything worked behind the scenes.

In the popular TV show *Happy Days*, which continues to play worldwide today, Ron epitomized everything naive and wholesome: the All-American ideal. The public always trusted his character, and he played it honestly. His likeability resonated a great deal with parents and teenagers alike. He was a great straight man for Fonzie, played by Henry Winkler.

In Chapter 6 there is much to be learned about how to approach working with a script, and Ron is a master at making it all look like the ideas and thoughts are coming out of his own head. That is truly the key in natural acting—and in comedy that is not as easy as it looks. It takes great practice, but it is well worth all of your hard work.

Valerie Harper

Valerie Harper became a huge success when she arrived on the television scene in *The Mary Tyler Moore Show,* which spun off her own TV series, *Rhoda.* This can happen when your character is so delicious that the public falls deeply in loves with it. Harper was a perfect compliment to Mary Tyler Moore. The viewer really believed their wonderful relationship. Although Valerie was born into a Protestant/Catholic family in Rockland County, New York, the world will always remember her as Rhoda Morgenstern, the Jewish girl who lived and worked in Manhattan. Her ability to perfect a believable accent and attitude was the cornerstone for her career. Working on dialects is a must, and I highly recommend it as a daily discipline. Valerie would work on a specific dialect at home and then spend time with people who spoke the same dialect in real life. It paid off, for Valerie won several Emmys and a Golden Globe for her efforts. Valerie's classic TV series set the stage for today's ensemble work in series like *Will & Grace,* and still remains popular for new generations in TV land.

Valerie had a strong improvisational background, as she had been with The Second City Improv Group, alongside her former husband Richard Shaal. I had the good fortune to interview Valerie a few times, and let me tell you, she's very likeable, energetic, warm, quick, and extremely talented as a comedic actress.

Lucille Ball

I worked with Lucille Ball at the end of her career on the 1989 Academy Awards show. She was a presenter, and I was coaching some of the presenters. She was a serious person in real life, and had a very low voice from her years of smoking. I played backgammon with her—trust me, she was a very serious player.

Lucy had been a B-actress in dramatic movies, and was as surprised as anyone else when she became a hot commodity in comedy. It just goes to show that you never know when comedy genius is going to hit! Lucy was an experimental comedienne, willing to make a fool of herself at the drop of a hat. Her genius at physical comedy is rare, and will be honored forever. It was an honor to be in the same room with her; she will make us laugh for a very long time. Use Lucy as a prime example of someone whose comedy brilliance didn't shine until she met the right person to complement it, which was—of course—Desi Arnaz.

Jerry Seinfeld

Jerry Seinfeld's comedy came strictly from the stand-up comedy world. Jerry was my guest on *The Paul Ryan Show*, and displayed to me his innate ability to bring a unique spin to his brilliant observational humor. He is wry, clean, wholesome, and makes the mundane funny. There was a time when a lot of agents, managers, and network executives were actively looking to build TV series around stand-ups. Jerry already had a great management team, who knew how to package a show successfully, leading Jerry to create one of the greatest TV comedies of all time.

Jerry's challenge was to learn to work with other actors, so he surrounded himself with very talented and experienced actors. As someone who always worked alone in his act, he now had to adapt to a new form of comedy. One of Jerry's hallmarks is nuance. His comedy involves the little, nitpicky details about life that people rarely think about. He taps into the everyday man with his humor, making the trivial magical.

Jackie Mason

Jackie Mason has worked for many years in stand-up, and has had success with his very popular one-person shows on Broadway. Jackie has always used his Jewish ethnicity to the hilt, brilliantly making it the basis for his comedy and bold observations on life. Jackie is disarming, and like Don Rickles, takes a lot of risks. Right off the cuff, he takes a simple fact and twists it, and it is hilarious. When I interviewed him, my parents picked him up and brought him to the television studio, as he doesn't drive. After finding out my mom is from England and my dad is from Philadelphia, he said to me, "Thank God your father went to England, because he couldn't get a date in all of America. Meanwhile, your mother was sitting alone in a room in England, with no one to go out with or talk to. Thank God your father went to England, and thank goodness they met each other!" He extends things to the absurd and paints a very funny picture for the audience.

INDEX